NOBLE EXERCISE

The Sporting Ideal in Eighteenth-Century British Art

Stephen Deuchar

"Hunting &c is a noble Exercise, and what most Country Gentlemen take great Delight in. . . ."

Complete Family-Piece, 1737, p. vii

Yale Center for British Art
New Haven, Connecticut 1982

Front cover: 1. David Allan: *Thomas Graham (afterwards 1st Baron Lynedoch) in Rome*, 1769

Back cover: 27. Daniel Lerpinière after John Wootton: *A Hunting Piece*, 1778

This catalogue is published on the occasion of an exhibition at the Yale Center for British Art, New Haven, Connecticut, July 14–September 19, 1982.

Copyright © 1982
by the Yale Center for British Art
Library of Congress Catalogue Card Number 82-050676
ISBN 0-930606-41-8

Printed in U.S.A.
at the direction of the Yale University Printing Service

Contents

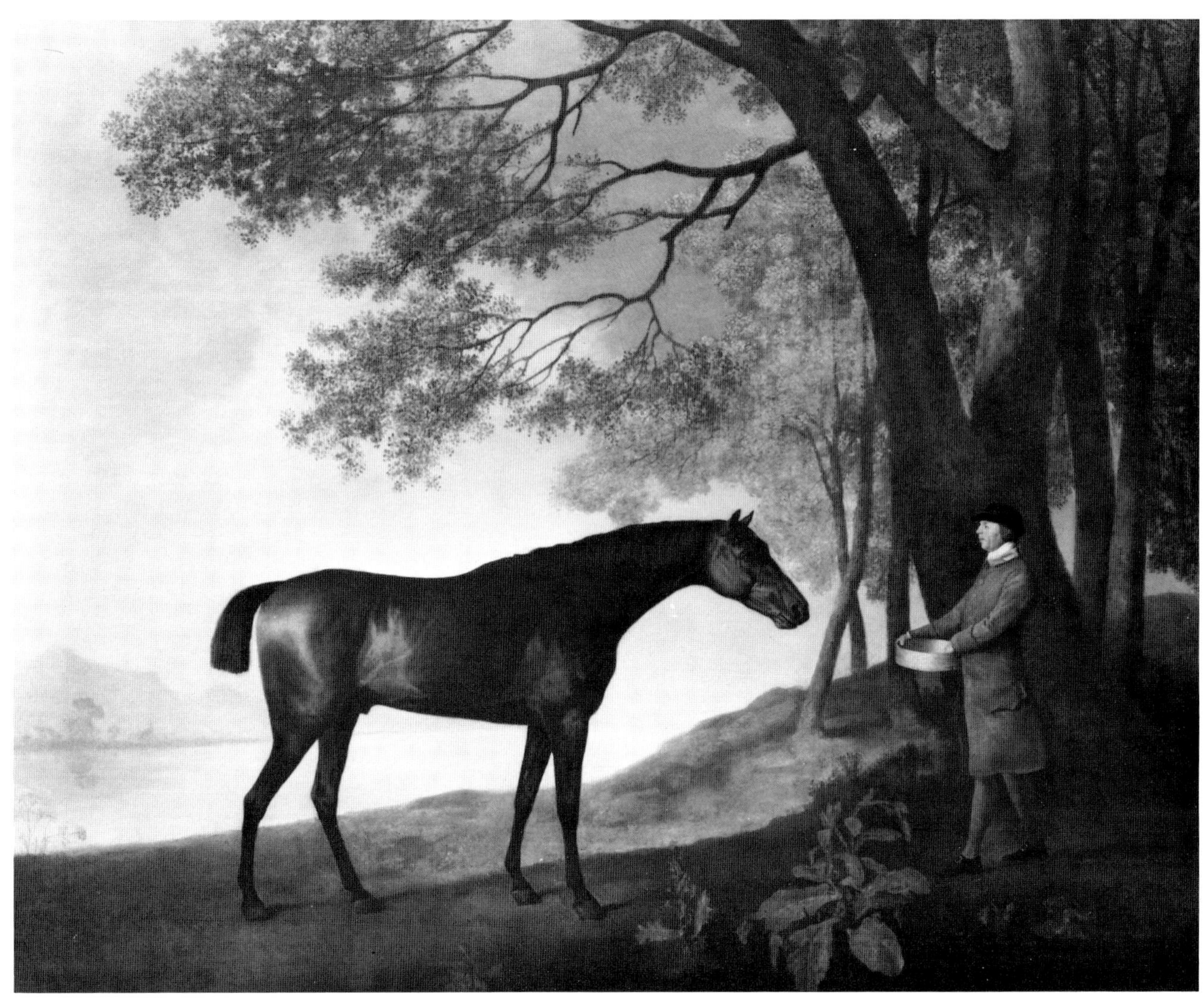

22. George Stubbs: *Shark with his Trainer Price*, 1775

Preface

Stephen Deuchar has been our Andrew W. Mellon Fellow in residence for the academic year 1981–82. He returns shortly to Westfield College, University of London, to continue his post-graduate research into eighteenth-century British sporting painting. His year at Yale has enabled him to further that cause, by giving him the opportunity to study the collections here and elsewhere in North America. In so doing, he has impressed us all with his knowledge of the subject and with the refreshing new insights he brings to bear upon it. We are particularly grateful to him for devoting a part of his time at the Center to the preparation of this exhibition; it provides our summer visitors with an opportunity to view an important group of works which are lent specifically for the show and to see them in the light of a lively and informative commentary.

Few subjects are as germane to the origins of the collection. The four canvases of the *Shooting* series (no. 20) which George Stubbs exhibited between 1767 and 1770 hang permanently in the Library Court. They serve as reminders that when Mr. Mellon acquired them, almost 200 years after they were painted, the reputation of Stubbs was at a low ebb. But as one "galloping Anglophile" extended his love of hunting from the field to the sale-room, others became infected, inevitably, by his taste and enthusiasm. As the subject of a forthcoming catalogue raisonné and a projected international exhibition, George Stubbs is one, and by no means the only example of the healthy revisionism which the Yale Center for British Art continues to engender. Stephen Deuchar's efforts belong to that same tradition, as he argues vigorously for wider appreciation of an art which, in spite of a certain popularity, has been consistently undervalued by scholars and museum curators. The exhibition provides its own form of noble exercise from which we, the spectators, may derive both pleasure and instruction.

Duncan Robinson
Director

Acknowledgments

I owe thanks to many individuals for their assistance and encouragement during the preparation of this exhibition. My first debts are to Paul Mellon, who has lent no less than 59 objects for the occasion, and to Duncan Robinson, who first suggested that I undertake the project.

Throughout my year at Yale I have relied much on the kindness and expertise of the staff at the British Art Center. From the Department of Paintings, Malcolm Cormack, Curator, has been a constant source of advice and I have drawn freely on his knowledge and experience; both he and Susan Casteras, Assistant Curator, read the draft of the catalogue and made useful criticisms; and Joy Pepe, Curatorial Assistant, worked conscientiously and with remarkable patience on both the exhibition and catalogue from their beginnings. From the Department of Prints and Drawings, I would like to thank Patrick Noon, Curator, and his assistants Angela Bailey, Paula Bartlett, and Randi Joseph for their consistent help, as well as Thomas Hill of the Reference Library. Timothy Goodhue, Registrar, organized the loans, photography, and wall labels, with the assistance of Marilyn Hunt, Michael Marsland, and Laura Prete; and further technical work was carried out by Timothy Balboni, Henry Bayer, Robert Meyers, Vincent Raucci, Don Rogers, and Eugene Saulino. I am also very grateful to Constance Clement for supervising the publication of the catalogue, which was edited by Lawrence Kenney and produced under the direction of the Yale University Printing Service.

Selection and shipping of objects from Mr. Mellon's collection at Upperville, Virginia, were facilitated by the efficiency of Beverly Carter, Mary Ann Thompson, Michelle Tompkins, and Eugene Howard; I would like to acknowledge in addition their thoughtful hospitality during my visit there in December 1981.

Of the many others who have given practical help or moral support, I wish to offer particular thanks to David Bindman, Judy Egerton, Joany Hichberger, Sarah Hyde, Antonia Lant, Thomas Michie, Angela Miller, Barbara Mulligan, and Bruce Robertson.

My greatest debt is to Katie Scott.

Stephen Deuchar

Introduction

The eighteenth century was a period of particular importance in the history of British rural sport. A marked expansion in the sporting activities of the landed classes was accompanied by two developments which made sport more than ever before a subject of public attention. The first was the establishment and growth of a British school of sporting art; the second was the proliferation of arguments, written from increasingly opposed standpoints, over the validity of sport as a pastime. In recent years sporting art has received considerable attention from historians of sport and mild interest from historians of art, but there has been little attempt to study it in relation to eighteenth-century attitudes to its subject matter. The intention behind the present exhibition and catalogue is to provide such a perspective.

The concern shown by eighteenth-century British artists and writers towards the subject of sport may be explained initially by the spread and institutionalization of sport itself during these years. In a century relatively undisturbed by war, leisure became a serious occupation. A boom in country house building—particularly between 1690 and 1760—was the most symbolic consequence of the social and economic prosperity found by many among the landed classes. Whether the builders were the old aristocracy or newly wealthy industrialists, the country life ethos flourished. For the fashionable, a London season of politics and parties and a country season of sport and retirement divided the year.[1] Hunting, horse racing, shooting, and fishing were undertaken with an open vigor that would have been considered impolitic in preceding Puritan years and indiscreet in subsequent Victorian times.

As Master of the Quorn Hunt, Hugo Meynell publicized the sport of fox hunting in the middle of the century and thereby encouraged a timely replacement for stag hunting, an activity hindered increasingly by a shortage of stags. By breeding hounds capable of keeping up with the speediest fox and by using his political and social connections to advertise the fact, Meynell revitalized a sport which had previously lacked both viability and social respectability. The great hunts—the Quorn, the Belvoir, the Pytchley—grew in prestige, and even before Henry Prince of Wales's public patronage of the sport, Peter Beckford could declare in 1781, "Fox hunting is now become the amusement of gentlemen, nor need any gentleman be ashamed of it."[2] The success of the sport was assured: foxes were vermin and therefore public enemies (church wardens were required by law to pay a reward for every fox killed in their parish), they were common, and they provided fast and exciting entertainment. Shooting and fishing required less organization but enjoyed equal attention; they were strictly regulated by increasingly severe and complex game laws.[3] To own shooting or fishing rights undoubtedly "argued social status," as one modern author has suggested,[4] but the primary motivation behind such legal control was both to ensure good sport and to assert the rights of property: a natural inclination of any landowning politician. Shooting, made more simple by technical advances in gun-making, was a popular and less frantic alternative to fox hunting. Fishing, another writer has argued,[5] was more of a light social amusement than a serious sport; but the game laws confirmed its importance, and Isaac Walton's *The Compleat Angler* had already endowed it with a 'scientific' status which paralleled that sought by other rural sports.

Horse racing in the eighteenth century, though not under the Georges the chosen "sport of Kings," underwent still greater expansion and change. By 1728 a semiofficial racing calendar was being published annually, providing some degree of coordination to a sport whose organization was still somewhat chaotic. In the second half of the century this progress was consolidated by the presence of the newly founded Jockey Club.[6] The Club's origins are obscure, as are its initial aims, but since its early membership included some of the richest and most influential men in the country, it naturally acquired prestige and, in time, a legal authority that gave the Turf a backbone which could support the establishment of major national events. By 1780 three of the Classic races (the Derby, the Oaks, and the St. Leger) had been founded, and the remaining two (the Two Thousand and One Thousand Guineas) followed early in the next century.

Sport was an expensive pastime, but its social base was broadening constantly. The introduction of subscription packs—packs of foxhounds maintained by groups of subscribers rather than by individuals—appeared towards the end of the century, allowing organized hunting to become accessible to the less affluent. The most consistently successful owners of racehorses tended to come from the ranks of the wealthy aristocracy, but race meetings were sporting events in which owners, jockeys, and gambling spectators from peerage to peasantry were all participants. The commission and purchase of sporting paintings, however, were largely the preserve of the wealthier classes. Their demand for pictorial representations of their leisure activity increased alongside its growth.

This 'documentary' function is conventionally regarded as the essence of British sporting art. Certainly many sporting pictures attempt to do no more than record a particular racing victory, hunting incident, or appearance of a particular horse. On such a level it may be argued that they parallel contemporary pictures of country houses or topographical landscapes through their apparent emphasis on accurate description. Francis Barlow (1626–1704), the first native-born artist to specialize in animal and sporting subjects, undoubtedly helped to establish a tradition of 'observation and record,' but the most popular sporting artists of the eighteenth century seem to have had wider intentions. While accurate delineation of animal flesh or sporting costume was generally required by expert sportsmen, the composition and setting of a sporting scene might be open to idealized or even fanciful interpretation. One of the aims of this exhibition is to show that such idealization was related to the ideal notions of sport expressed in literary form, but pictorial influences were naturally of direct importance. John Wootton (1683?–1764) was a prominent figure in the early history of British sporting painting. Although he produced several exact and unadventurous horse portraits, the influence of his Dutch master Jan Wyck (*ca.* 1645–1700) and his evident interest in the art of Claude and Gaspard place many of his sporting pictures far outside the realm of topography. Wootton's development of the 'sporting conversation piece' and his attempts at large-scale decorative schemes are further evidence of his range and ambition. James Seymour (1702–52), who "was thought even superior to Wootton in drawing a horse,"[7] followed many of Wootton's formulas but created a still less descriptive and strangely simplified style: stables are unnaturally clean; dogs and horses walk in step. There is an air of almost disturbing artificiality in composition and mood which to some extent influenced George Stubbs (1724–1806). Though deeply committed to the observation of animal anatomy, Stubbs tended to avoid a purely narrative or documentary approach to the portrayal of sport, and followers such as Sawrey Gilpin (1733–1807) even attempted a synthesis of animal and history painting.[8]

But whatever the evidence that much sporting art did more than simply record sport, its reputation as an inferior category of art has a long and apparently persuasive history. Low in the hierarchy of artistic worthiness (a scale defined most clearly by the French Academy in the seventeenth century and later underlined in Reynolds's *Discourses*),[9] sporting painting was destined to be categorized among those "kinds of pictures which can do no more than please."[10] For John Byng, later 5th Viscount Torrington, this was no bad thing:

> Surely the intention of paintings was to chear the mind, and restore your pleasures;—to survey your ancestry with conscious esteem;—to view the beauties of nature; to restore the memory of famous horses, and of faithful dogs.[11]

This attitude would have exasperated such men as James Barry, who in 1773 was pleading for a "solid manly taste for real art, in the place of our trifling and contemptible passion for the daubing of little inconsequential things—portraits of dogs, landscapes &c."[12] And though sporting art could evidently command high prices (John Wootton asked quite as much for his horse portraits as did his illustrious contemporary Sir Godfrey Kneller for human portraits, and George Stubbs's prices may be compared to those of Sir Joshua Reynolds),[13] this tended to attract some practitioners whose level of competence did little to enhance its reputation. The general belief that connoisseurs of sport could not also be connoisseurs of art was a further hindrance: Edward Edwards was to write of Richard Roper (*ca.* 1730–*ca.* 1775), "his powers as an artist were not considerable, yet sufficient to satisfy the gentlemen of the turf and the stable."[14] Certainly there is evidence of a general disdain for sporting artists in Stubbs's desire to lose his label as a "horse-painter" and in the irony of "Peter Pindar's" (Dr. Wolcott's) comments on this:

> 'Tis said that naught so much the temper rubs,
> Of that ingenious artist Mr. Stubbs,
> As calling him a horse-painter—how strange,
> That Stubbs the title should desire to change![15]

According to Henry Angelo (1760–1839?), Stubbs's achievement was to "raise the reputation" of sporting art, which we may therefore assume was low; nonetheless, Angelo adds, "Stubbs's rare and recondite talent was not understood in the age in which he lived."[16]

Sportsmen with little understanding of art and art critics with little interest in sport seem to have been responsible both in the past and today for assigning either too great or too small an importance to British sporting art. For Theodore Cook, the art, like the sport, symbolizes "the racial pluck and stamina of Englishman and Scot," and, he observes, "that man would be a dull dog indeed whose blood was not fired . . . by such vivid scenes of pleasure."[17] For Ellis Waterhouse, "to discuss the Sartorius tribe and such painters is no business of the historian of art, no matter how bitter the accusations of neglect are wont to be from those specialist writers who sometimes confuse the history of art with praising famous horses."[18] Such extremities of opinion reflect sporting art's insoluble problem: sport, unlike the human figure or trees or fields, is controversial subject matter even before it reaches the canvas. Sportsmen are liable to exaggerate the worth of a sporting painting if they associate personal experience with its content; non-sportsmen, if they are critical or even just apathetic about what it describes, may be contemptuous. For this reason sporting art is most fairly viewed within the context of the critical and defensive attitudes its subject matter naturally provokes. This catalogue explores the nature and the range of the attitudes in the eighteenth century which surrounded the patronage and production of the works of art in the exhibition. Before we examine in detail the grounds on which sport was justified and denounced, a few introductory remarks may be made on the general basis of the disagreement.

Since defenders of sport tended to live in the country and critics in the town, the conflict should be seen initially as part of the wider confrontation between rural and urban ideologies.[19] *The Sportsman's Evening Brush*, 1792, an anthology of eighteenth-century hunting songs, provides evidence of this:

> Let the drudge of the town make riches his sport
> And the slave of the state hunt the smiles of the court.
> No care nor ambition *our* patience annoy,
> But innocence still gives a zest to our joy. . . .[20]

Meanwhile Lord Chesterfield was to urge the polite recreations of "dancing, fencing and elegant horsemanship" (that might be practiced in London or Bath) above "the rustick and illiberal sports of gun, dogs, and horse,"[21] despite sportsmen's objections that city fops knew nothing of sport and therefore should not presume to judge it. The "Country Squire" who wrote *An Essay on Hunting*, 1733, complained,

> Balls and Operas, Assemblies and Masquerades so exhaust the Spirits of the puny Creatures over Night, that Yawning and Chocolate are the main Labours and Entertainments of the Morning. . . . what Wonder then if such busy, trifling, effeminate Mortals are heard to swear they have no Notion of venturing their Bodies out of Doors on the cold Air of the Morning? I have laught heartily to see such delicate Smock faced Animals judiciously interrupting their Pinches of Snuff with dull Jokes upon Fox-Hunters.[22]

Much later in the century John Byng expressed similar impatience: "I do experience (with peevishness sometimes) the plumpest opposition on the subjects of hunting, wine &c from those who never sported and only drank water."[23] And while Byng's bracketing of "hunting" with "wine" reflected the view that on one level at least sport was justifiable merely because it was enjoyable, this only constituted grounds for criticism by others. The notion that sportsmen were ill-mannered revellers was summarized by Daniel Defoe, who saw a country squire to be one who "hunts, hawkes, shootes, and follows his game, hallows to his dogs, dams his servants, dotes upon his horses, drinks with his huntsmen . . . is talkative . . . intollerable . . . dogmatic."[24] Fielding's Squire Western of course did little to correct this image. In both cases the primary object of criticism or satire was the landed classes rather than sport itself, but such commentaries unavoidably did much to surround sport with an aura of irrationality and excess.

Indeed, much of the objection to sport stemmed from its apparently excessive, and thus impolite, indulgence. The objection could be expressed in light parody, as in *Newmarket, or an Essay on the Turf*, 1771:

> I lost my mistress, horse, and wife,
> But when I think on human life,
> I'm glad it is no worse;
> My mistress was grown lean and old,
> My wife was ugly and a scold,
> —I'm sorry for my horse.[25]

—or in a more serious form, as in a letter to the *Gentleman's Magazine* in 1734 which declared, "The Chace, which was an elegant Refreshment to our forefathers, is so degenerated that their successors seem as if they thought they were born for no other purpose."[26] John of Salisbury's remarks on the excesses of hunting made some 600 years earlier suggest that this correspondent was being falsely nostalgic,[27] but certainly there was little consistent criticism of sport until the seventeenth century. In the late sixteenth and early seventeenth centuries Gervase Markham's voluminous writings on sport—timely recommendations of an activity then being given particular prominence by its royal patronage—may perhaps be seen as opening the debate with their thorough stress on the 'noble' and health-giving properties of sport and on its 'patriotic' use as a training ground for war.[28] That it was also enjoyable brought Puritan reaction and the accusation that it was a vice:

> If we shall come in to a house, and see many Physic-boxes and Glasses we should conclude somebody is sick; so when we see Hounds, and Hawks, and Cards, and Dice, we may fear that there is some sick soul in that family[29]

wrote John Dod. Horse racing was even banned during the régime of the Major-Generals, but on the grounds that public gatherings might bring "the great confluence of irreconcilable enemies"[30] rather than through any moral objection. Calmer social conditions in the following century accompanied, as we have seen, an expansion in sporting activity, and thus the inevitable crystallization of arguments over its worth.

The relationship between sporting art and this written discussion is the concern of much of the following essay. It does not attempt to make a general survey of sporting art of the period, to examine artistic influences in detail, or to provide biographical information. Such ground has recently been covered in the series *Sport in Art and Books: The Paul Mellon Collection*. Individual works in the exhibition are catalogued and discussed in the following four volumes: Judy Egerton, *British Sporting and Animal Paintings 1655–1867*, 1978; Judy Egerton and Dudley Snelgrove, *British Sporting and Animal Drawings 1500–1850*, 1978; Dudley Snelgrove, *British Sporting and Animal Prints 1658–1874*, 1981; and John B. Podeschi, *Books on the Horse and Horsemanship 1400–1941*, 1981. The present writer's debt to these scholars is considerable, for an exploration of alternative avenues can only begin safely from the wide factual base established by their research. This exhibition provides the opportunity to explore one such avenue in an area of British art that is represented comprehensively in the Paul Mellon Collection.

Notes

1. A basic but perceptive account of English eighteenth-century social and economic history may be found in E. N. Williams, *Life in Georgian England* (London, 1962).

2. Peter Beckford, *Thoughts upon Hunting* (Sarum, 1781), p. 177.

3. See *A Dialogue between a Lawyer and a Country Gentleman upon the Subject of the Game Laws* (London, 1771), and E. P. Thompson, *Whigs and Hunters* (London, 1975).

4. J. H. Plumb, *The Pursuit of Happiness* (Yale Center for British Art exhibition catalogue, 1977), p. 25.

5. Stella A. Walker, *Sporting Art* (London, 1972), p. 87.

6. See Roger Mortimer, *The Jockey Club* (London, 1958).

7. Horace Walpole, *Anecdotes of Painting in England*, ed. J. Dallaway and R. N. Wornum, (New York, 1969), Vol. 2, p. 329.

8. Concise summaries of the lives and works of sporting painters represented in this exhibition may be found in Judy Egerton, *British Sporting and Animal Paintings 1655–1867* (London, 1978).

9. See Rensselaer W. Lee, *Ut Pictura Poesis: The Humanistic Theory of Painting* (New York, 1967), pp. 18–19.

10. J. Richardson, *Works* (London, 1773), p. 117, from the *Art of Criticism* (London, 1719).

11. The Hon. John Byng (later 5th Viscount Torrington), *The Torrington Diaries 1781–1794*, ed. C. B. Andrews (London, 1935), Vol. 2, p. 139.

12. Quoted in John Pye, *Patronage of British Art* (London, 1845), p. 214.

13. See Walter Shaw Sparrow, *British Sporting Artists from Barlow to Herring*, 2nd ed. (London, 1965), pp. 93–94.

14. Edward Edwards, *Anecdotes of Painters* (London, 1808), p. 11.

15. Quoted in Constance-Anne Parker, *Mr. Stubbs the Horse Painter* (London, 1971), p. 108.

16. Henry Angelo, *Reminiscences* (London, 1828–30), Vol. 1, pp. 29–30.

17. *Sporting Pictures at Lavington Park*, privately printed 1927, introduction by Sir Theodore Cook, pp. viii, x.

18. Ellis Waterhouse, *Painting in Britain 1530–1790*, 4th ed. (Harmondsworth, 1978), p. 297.

19. See, for example, *The Spectator*, nos. 119–31, July, 1711.

20. *The Sportsman's Evening Brush* (London, 1792), p. 31.

21. Quoted in G. E. Mingay, *English Landed Society in the Eighteenth Century* (London and Toronto, 1963), p. 153.

22. *An Essay on Hunting, by a Country Squire* (London, 1733), pp. 5–6.

23. Byng, *Torrington Diaries*, p. 173.

24. Daniel Defoe, *The Complete English Gentleman* (1730), ed. K. D. Bülbring (London, 1890), p. 39.

25. *Newmarket, or an Essay on the Turf* (London, 1771), Vol. 2, p. 103.

26. *The Gentleman's Magazine* (March 1734), pp. 154–55.

27. See John of Salisbury (Bishop of Chartres, born *ca.* 1120), *Policratus*, bk. 1, ed. Joseph B. Pike (Massachusetts, 1938), p. 18.

28. See, for example, Gervase Markham, *Country Contentments* (London, 1616).

29. Quoted in William Haller, *The Rise of Puritanism* (New York, 1938), p. 59.

30. Major Whalley to Cromwell, quoted in Dennis Brailsford, *Sport and Society* (London and Toronto, 1969), p. 138.

I. The Celebration of Sport

Hunting it is the noblest exercise,
Makes men laborious, active, wise,
Brings health, and does the spirits delight,
It helps the hearing and the sight:
It teacheth arts that never slip
The memory, good horsemanship,
Search, sharpness, courage, and defence,
And chaseth all ill habits thence.

Ben Jonson, *Time Vindicated to Himself and to His Honors*, 1623, ll. 412–19

Favorable descriptions of sport in eighteenth-century literature were expressed in a particular language which both reflected old and created new notions of the benefits of sport. Quite specific themes become identifiable through their recurrence, constituting elements of what may be called a 'sporting ideal'. Jonson's words above summarize the ideal as it stood in the early seventeenth century: hunting is noble and aids health and work, horsemanship and military skill. In the eighteenth century these notions and further ones were expressed more expansively, partly in response to the growth of sport and partly in response to criticism of it. The relationship between this written ideology and sporting art was unavoidably close. On one level the visual imagery depended on the literature. For example, in the case of a portrait where a sporting gun is included the spectator was asked to associate the sitter with the traditional and ideal qualities of sportsmen that had been developed most coherently in literary form. Thus the gun held by Windham Quin (cat. no. 10) implies that its owner is laborious, active, wise, and so forth. On another level the pictorial form could bolster the existing body of ideology: a sportsman portrayed as a notably capable horseman, as in Jan Wyck's *Hare Hunting* (cat. no. 28), would automatically encourage a connection between sport and good horsemanship, effectively providing visual evidence of the written notion.

It would be unwise to assume that any sporting picture had a particular literary parallel, but it is certainly true that the assumptions artists made about sport were inevitably related to the attitudes of the society in which they lived, and that these attitudes were most unambiguously articulated in a literary form. By drawing from a large selection of written sources it is possible to bring to light the nature and the constituents of the sporting ideal and to explore its manifestation and perpetuation in paintings, prints, and drawings.

The link between sport and health is stressed in the majority of eighteenth-century sporting books and alluded to in many pictures of hunting or shooting. "I shall . . . among the Benefits of the Chase give first Place to Health"[1] wrote the author of *An Essay on Hunting*, and indeed the health-giving properties of sport were usually emphasized above all others. On the simplest level sport was recommended on medical grounds. An early appearance of this theme in England was in Sir Thomas Elyot's *The Governor* of 1531: "by exercise, which is a vehement motion (as Galen, prince of physicians defineth) the health of man is preserved and his strength increased."[2] In the following century, Henry Peacham was more specific:

> Shooting is also a very healthfull and commendable recreation for Gentlemen; neither do I know any other comparable unto it for stirring every part of the body; for it openeth the breast and pipes, excerciseth the armes and feete, and with less violence than running, leaping & c.[3]

In the eighteenth century there tended to be less emphasis on the medical aspect and more on the generally healthful advantages of a sporting life, often contrasted to an 'unhealthy' city life. "Fly the rank city, shun its turbid air!"[4] urged one poet who was extolling the virtues of sport in 1744, and John Careless recounted early in the following century—with rather less gravity—the story of one Jemmy Graceful, who

> Chose to live out of town because it was healthful;
> Rather fattish and short, he talk much of sporting,
> Kept his dog and his gun, with all that sort of thing.[5]

Certain eighteenth-century sporting pictures were evidently thought by contemporaries to suggest or reflect a similar connection between sport and health. When the prints after Stubbs's four shooting scenes (see cat. nos. 20, 21) were published, they were accompanied by verses which may be seen as reliable indications of the light in which the pictures were interpreted, and even of the spirit in which they were painted. Of the first scene is written:

> Lo! the keen Sportsmen rise from Beds of Down
> And quit the Environs of the Smoaky Town
>
> Whate'er the Pleasures of the coming Day
> Secure of Health they Jocund walk away.[6]

The healthiness of early rising was itself a common theme and should be seen as one implication of any other sporting picture in which an early morning setting is portrayed, as for example in James Seymour's *Mr. Peter Delmé's Hounds on the Hampshire Downs*, 1738 (cat. no. 19). Furthermore, William Cobbet's preference for field sports over "all other pastimes because they produce early rising, because they have a tendency to lead young men into virtuous habits"[7] is evidence of a trend of thought which linked early rising with virtue. Peter Delmé might well have hoped that a spectator of Seymour's picture would think along similar lines. There is less need for speculation, however, over the intention of Thomas Rowlandson's *Four o'clock in the Country*, 1788 (cat. no. 64), in which the virtue of rural early rising is plainly indicated through contrast with

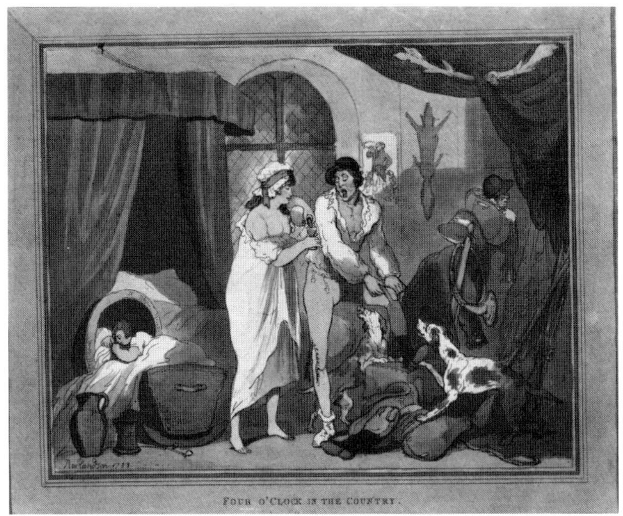

64. Thomas Rowlandson: *Four o'clock in the Country*, 1788

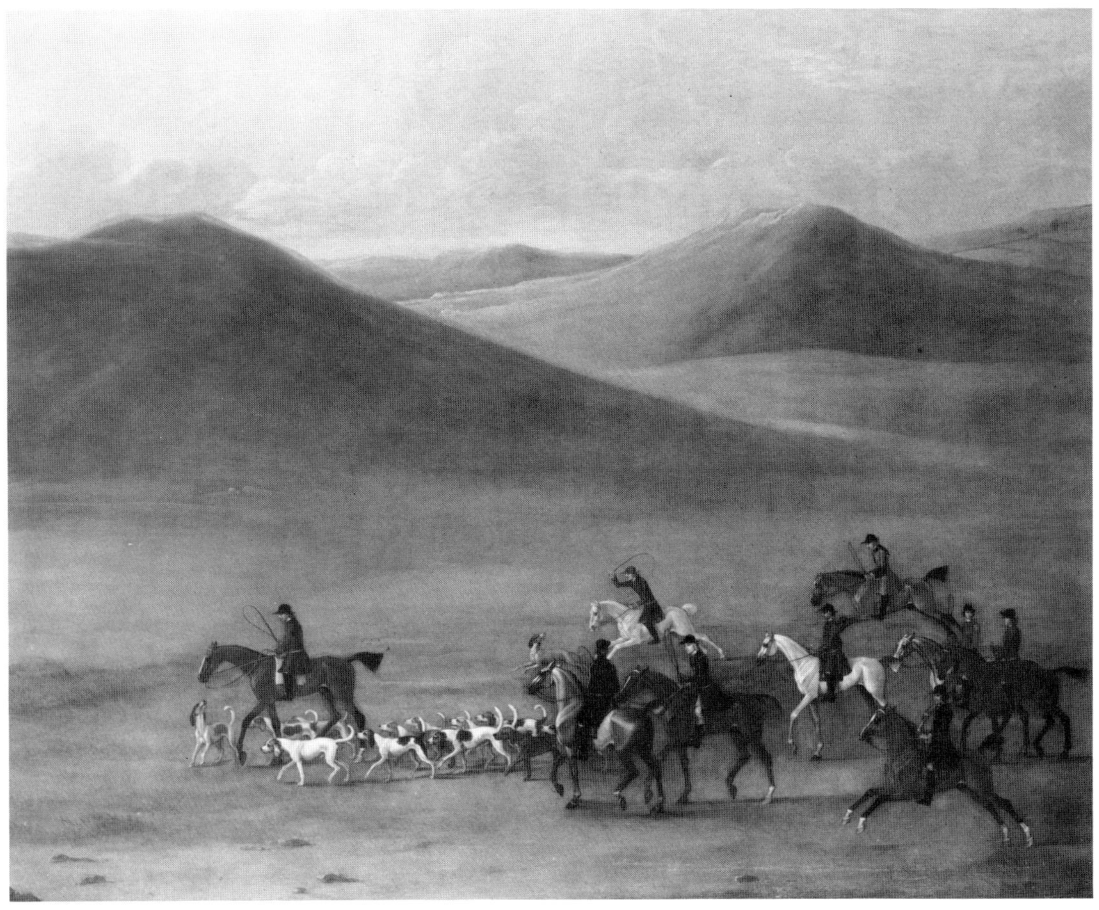

19. James Seymour: *Mr. Peter Delmé's Hounds on the Hampshire Downs*, 1738

the companion piece, *Four o'clock in Town*, 1788 (cat. no. 65): at the hour at which the sportsman rises from bed dutifully—if a little reluctantly—for early morning sport, his somewhat dazed urban counterpart prepares for bed after a late night of distinctly unvirtuous revelry.

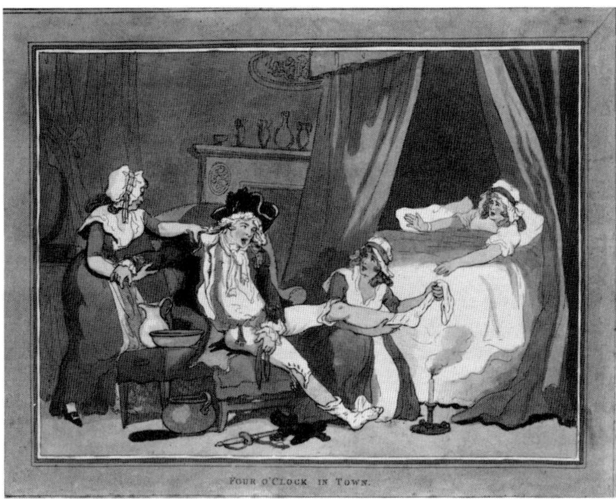

65. Thomas Rowlandson:
Four o'clock in Town, 1788

"The morning is charming, all nature is gay"[8] began one typical eighteenth-century hunting song. Quite as important as any connection with virtue was that early rising allowed nature to be experienced most thoroughly. The reassessment of man's relationship with nature was of course a pervasive feature of eighteenth-century culture.[9] It helps to explain the popularity of the outdoor portrait from which one branch of sporting art developed. The precise way in which the sporting ideal was located within this wider context becomes evident in the following extract from the introduction to the *Sportsman's Dictionary*, a work first published in 1735 and reprinted many times during the century:

> The diversions that are the subject of these volumes . . . are so peculiarly adapted to scenes of rural life, that a just knowledge of them is considered as a necessary accomplishment in gentlemen, who devote their vacant hours to the country.
>
> It would be needless to enlarge on the satisfactions and advantages they are capable of affording us. No prospect of nature can awake more pleasing ideas in the imagination, than a landscape, distributed into verdant woods, and opening lawns, with the diversity of extended plains, flowery meadows, and clear streams; the heart of the contemplative beholder melts into secret raptures at this inchanting view, and he is immediately prompted to hail the great benefactor who sheds such a profusion of beauties around him. But when he likewise regards them as so many rich magazines, intended for the accommodation of his table, as well as for the improvement of his health, and the solace of his mind, he begins to think it a reproach to him to be unacquainted with the manner of acquiring these enjoyments that were created for his use with so much liberality; and he is then convinced that Hunting, Fowling, Fishing, and Riding, are more necessary to his welfare, than he might at first imagine.[10]

This idea of sport as a means of both enjoying and exploiting nature is indicated in many sporting pictures, particularly those in which landscape is treated with as much or more attention than sporting activity. John Henry Muntz's watercolor of *Landscape with Sportsmen and Dogs Resting*, 1779 (cat. no. 14), may be seen either as a landscape in which the sportsmen are decorative *staffage* or as a sporting picture in which the expanse and beauty of the sportsmen's environment is emphasized. In either case sport and landscape are assumed to be mutually complementary. In artistic terms this forms part of a tradition which was best known in eighteenth-century England through seventeenth-century Dutch painting and which derived ultimately from medieval hunting tapestries, but contemporary literary discussion of sport, landscape, and their relationship had a more immediate influence on eighteenth-century taste. Thomas Rowlandson's *A Stag Hunt in the West Country* (cat. no. 16), for example, owes little to immediate artistic precedent, but by the pictorial fusion of sporting activity with surrounding nature it expresses succinctly a crucial element in the current sporting ideal.

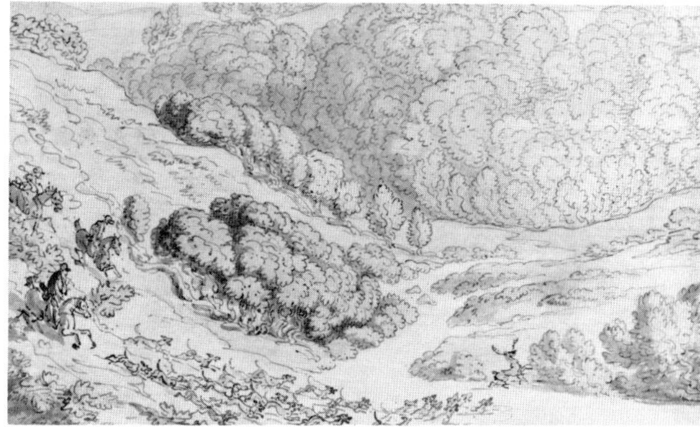

16. Thomas Rowlandson:
A Stag Hunt in the West Country

A related literary theme was that of sport and relaxation as a necessary balance to work and business. Sometimes this too was linked to the town/country issue and the idea of 'retirement': the author of the *Complete Family-Piece* of 1737 wished to discuss rural sports "for

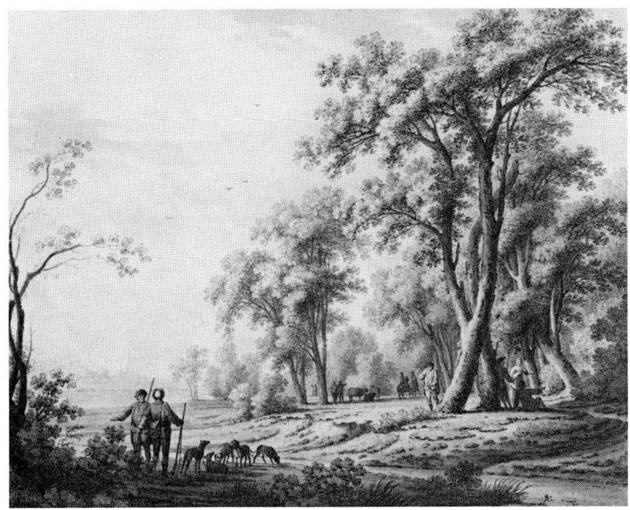

14. John Henry Muntz: *Landscape with Sportsmen and Dogs Resting*, 1779

the Benefit and Advantage . . . of such Gentlemen who retire from Business to live in the Country."[11] Before the eighteenth century the interrelationship of sport and business tended to be argued more simply in terms of the former providing a refreshing and restorative break from the latter. "Repose is sought after Labor"[12] stated John of Salisbury in the twelfth century: a straightforward and persuasive justification for sport which was repeated widely in subsequent centuries. Furthermore, Richard Brathwait's belief that "continuall or incessant imployment cannot be endured, there must be some intermission or the bodie becomes enfeebled" implied that sport was not merely a justifiable pastime but an essential one.[13]

In the eighteenth century there were one or two modifications to this theme which reflect the association elsewhere of sport with idleness. For Lord Chesterfield pleasure was indeed a necessary corollary to efficient work, but, he stressed, it should be seen only in relation to the work that preceded it. "No man tastes pleasures truly who does not earn them by previous business,"[14] he argued, although he was of a social class that had ample opportunity for recreation without the need to work first. Others would suggest, perhaps with more honesty, that if a person did not need to work he should make a business out of recreation and thereby combat the temptation to be idle. The "Country Squire" of 1733 urged sport on such moral grounds: "Idleness is the Parent of Mischief: one who has nothing to do is expos'd to every Temptation, and stands at Sale (like a Beast in the Market) to the first Bidder, the *World* or the *Devil*."[15] Typical of early eighteenth-century middle-class morality, this attitude had seen fuller and more ironic expression in *The Spectator*:

> Manufactures, trade, and agriculture, naturally employ more than nineteen parts of the species in twenty; and as for those who are not obliged to labour, by the condition in which they are born, they are more miserable than the rest of mankind, unless they indulged themselves in that voluntary labour which goes by the name of exercise. My friend Sir Roger [Sir Roger de Coverley, *The Spectator's* fictional sportsman] has been an indefatigable man in business of this kind, and has hung several parts of his house with the trophies of his former labours.[16]

By this logic it might be argued that to take part in sporting activity was to display proof of one's leisured status; thus one of a sporting picture's attractions to its patron might be that it supplied a record of that proof. In this way pictures would become an equivalent of Sir Roger's "trophies," by indicating both that their owner did not need to work and that he avoided idleness. Alternatively, if the patron did have to work for a living the presence of a sporting picture on the wall could imply to a visitor the patron's probable efficiency in that work. Moreover, the precise content of a picture could suggest a specific contrast between work and leisure. While no clear cases exist of artists implying directly that sport was a necessary corollary to business—indeed this would be difficult to suggest visually—pictures in which both sportsmen and peasant workers are shown together (as in *Bifrons Park*, *ca.* 1705–10, cat. no. 2, ill. p. 14), unavoidably stress the former's social status which allows their leisure.

The association between sport and social status was at the heart of the sporting ideal. Since sport was a means of testing and practicing equestrian skills, the traditional identification of royalty with horsemanship contributed to the view of sport as "noble exercise." Related in origin to concepts of knightly chivalry and the cult of the courtier, this theme gained notable ground in seventeenth-century England. Horsemanship was an attribute of "Kings and princes whose delight in ancient times was to ride and manage great horses," wrote Henry Peacham in 1622 (and indeed it was in this era that royal seals showing the royal family on horseback first appeared in England[17]). Therefore "Hawking and hunting . . . are recreations very commendable and befitting a noble or gentleman to exercise,"[18] continued Peacham, showing, in his assumption that behavior could create or provide evidence of 'nobility', a concern which was to assume great importance in the eighteenth century.

Social fluidity and the decline of the monarchy's polit-

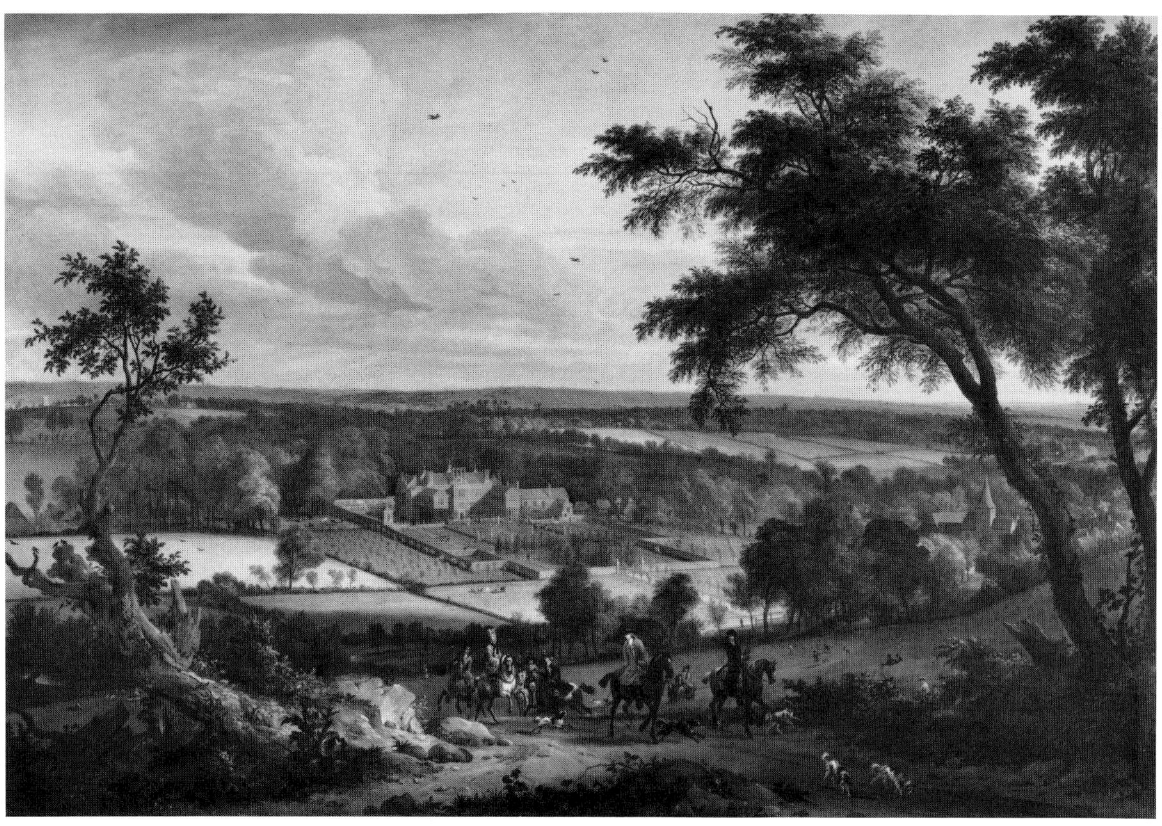

2. British School: *Bifrons Park, ca.* 1705–10

ical power (and thus social influence) brought a new ethic of 'nobility', which though superseding traditional courtly ideals inevitably bore their traces. The nobility of sport was argued in three principal ways. The first was the most general. Because sport implied excitement and courage, it was said to stir the imagination and to bring thoughts of ancient deeds of heroism: a loose form of nobility based on antiquity. Books on sport invariably began by stressing its ancient origins and doubtless influenced spectators such as Daniel Defoe, who described how he "diverted [himself] in a . . . noble Manner" at Newmarket by imagining himself "in the Circus Maximus at Rome, seeing . . . the Races of the Chariots and Horsemen."[19] The Earl of Bath, likewise, judged horse racing to be "a noble sight . . . a piece of grandeur."[20] The fabled nobility of the horse naturally contributed to such interpretations. The verses which accompanied one of England's earliest sporting prints, Barlow's *The Last Horse Race run before Charles II . . . at Datchett Ferry,* 1687,[21] related how the "noble Bruites" strove heroically for victory, and certainly many sporting pictures would have been seen to suggest the nobility of sport or of its human and animal participants. The perhaps absurdly heroic stance of the animals in Thomas Weaver's *Coursing,* 1800 (cat. no. 23), clearly forwards the idea that the sportsmen are engaged in an activity of considerable dignity; and even such a potentially mundane subject as horses in a stable could be given a deliberate air of nobility by an artist if animals and environment were presented in a sufficiently idealized manner. In *The Stables and Two Famous Running Horses Belonging to the Duke of Bolton,* 1747 (cat. no. 17), James Seymour aims at such ennoblement by unapologetically creating a wholly artificial cleanliness and sense of order.

The second aspect of the nobility of sport was expressed in relation to social class. The very concept of nobility needed reassessment in the eighteenth century, partly because money was becoming a stronger social force than birth:

> Wealth, howsoever got, in England makes
> Lords of mechanics, gentlemen of rakes;
> Antiquity and birth are needless here
> 'Tis impudence and money makes a peer . . .[22]

complained Defoe. Naturally both the newly rich and the threatened old aristocracy sought to associate themselves with traditional symbols of nobility that might enhance or confirm their social standing. Since sport was one such symbol, its noble and exclusive status was emphasized strongly. The elegant figures in *The Death of the Hare, ca.* 1765–70 (cat. no. 12), are as noble as the imaginary classical landscape in which they stand. The overtly idealized scene makes no concession to the chaotic reality of the climax of a hunt, but describes these ladies' and gentlemen's pastime in the same terms as writers who sought to connect sport with nobility. John Wootton's similarly grandiose scene, *Preparing for the Hunt, ca.* 1740–50 (cat. no. 26), was evidently painted in the same spirit, but, by contrasting the extravagant architecture and rather pretentious poses of some of the figures with the ragged foreground servant,[23] extends the noble and class associations of sport. Wootton's friend William Somerville likewise reminded his readers that hunting was "for the weak too strong, too costly for the poor,"[24] and the "Country Squire" had gloated in 1733 that "The Vulgar cannot have the least Notion of these noble Entertainments."[25] Or, as an amateur poet put it in the *Gentleman's Magazine* in 1734:

> Our laws prohibit hunting
> To the Plebian race;
> Nor is it meet the vulgar
> Should royal sports debace.[26]

Thirdly, the nobility of sport was argued in terms of manliness. Sport had long been seen as "savouring of manhood and gentry,"[27] but, partly in relation to the town/country dialogue, in the eighteenth century it was specifically contrasted with the courtly life that had once been its essence.

> How far superior are the rural sports
> To ease inglorious, or the Toil of Courts!
> From these proceeds up an Indolence supine;
> From those arises all that's masculine.[28]

wrote the author of *Hounslow Heath* in 1747, and J. Brown, in *An Estimate of the Manners and Principles of the Times*, 1757, added with regret that "The Manly Exercise of Riding is generally disused as too coarse and indelicate for the Fine Gentleman."[29] To the sportsman, sport was "noble and heroick" because it was one of "those Manly toils which laid the Foundation of Prowess and Glory in the ancient Heroes"[30] and which polite society had apparently forgotten. Effeminacy was seen by some to be the greatest modern evil, and the practice of sport might go at least some way to combat it.[31] Although sporting art forwarded the idea of manliness only in general terms, some artists did attempt to draw comparisons between sport and war. War, supposedly the epitome of manliness, was itself an important constituent of the sporting ideal.

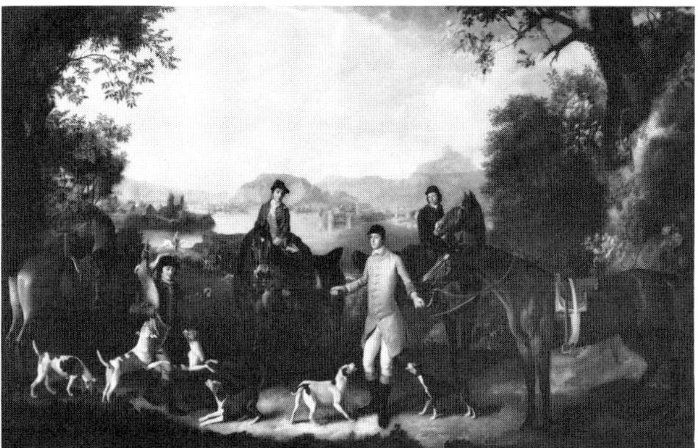
12. British School: *The Death of the Hare, ca.* 1765–70

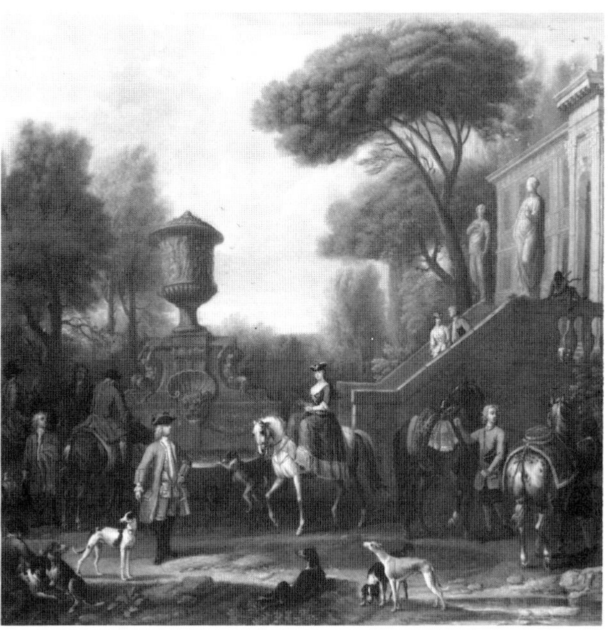
26. John Wootton:
Preparing for the Hunt, ca. 1740–50

The theoretical function of sport as a training ground for war has a long history. Henry Peacham was not the first to cite the opinion of Eusebius that "wild beasts were of purpose created by God that men by chasing and encountering them might be fitted and enabled for warlike exercises."[32] The strategy involved in pursuing and capturing animals, it was argued, provided good practice for evolving military strategy, and the physical fitness that sport stimulated also aided stamina in battle. Good horsemanship was an essential ingredient in the art of war, and this too would be encouraged by sport. Dr. Johnson explained in his introduction to Somerville's *The Chace* that "hunting was the exercise of the greatest heroes in antiquity. By this they formed themselves for war; and their exploits against wild beasts were a prelude to their other victories."[33] This was perhaps by way of explanation of the poet's presentation of sport as an heroic and distinctly warlike activity in itself; Somerville's description of otter hunting, for example, is alarmingly enthusiastic:

> Bid the loud horns in gayly warbling strains
> Proclaim the felon's fate; he dies, he dies!
> Rejoice ye scaly tribes and leaping dance
> Above the wave in sign of liberty
> Restor'd. The cruel tyrant is no more![34]

For some men, perhaps, a natural urge for blood and excitement (which Thomas Bewick discussed sadly later in the century)[35] would be satisfied by sport when a war was not available, but the sporting ideal clung persistently throughout the eighteenth century to the notion that sport was in some sense a patriotic activity. As Master of the Epping Hunt, Colonel Thomas Thornton's pseudomilitary sporting costume may have raised some eyebrows,[36] but a contemporary hunting toast roundly declared "May the enemies of Britain ever prove a main object of every sportsman's pursuit."[37]

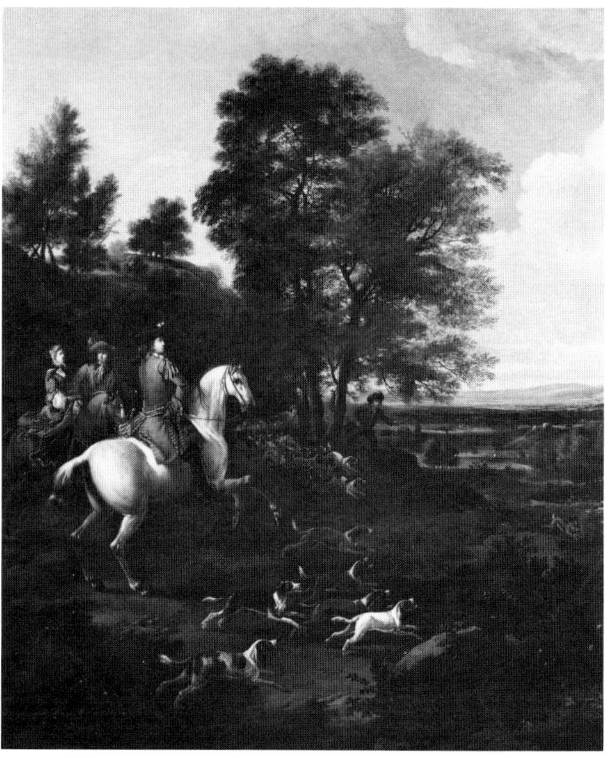

28. Jan Wyck: *Hare Hunting, ca.* 1690

Sporting art could also stir patriotic feelings in the minds of spectators. *Blackwoods Magazine* wrote in 1824 of Henry Alken: "It is he that can . . . show you the feats in the field of those who are destined hereafter to shake the arsenal." Such a response may have been encouraged more by the contemporary political climate than by the precise content of Alken's work, but in the previous century certain artists seem to have drawn more deliberate parallels between sport and war. Early sporting painters working in England, such as Tillemans, Wyck, and Wootton, were also employed as painters of battle scenes. Since battles and hunts had many features in common—horses, men, fields, and a good deal of excitement—it is perhaps inevitable that painters of one should be called on to paint the other, and that the two kinds of pictures should bear certain similarities. But in the light of the strong ideal association between sport and war, and sportsmen's understandable liking for seeing themselves portrayed as heroes, it must be assumed that certain sporting scenes were actually intended to resemble battle scenes. Jan Wyck's elegant horseman in *Hare Hunting, ca.* 1690 (cat. no. 28) seems designed to appear as much like a general as a huntsman, and indeed, Judy Egerton has pointed out that the same pose is to be found in Wyck's battle scenes.[38] Egerton has also suggested that John Wootton derived the poses of the King and the Earl of Orford in *George I at Newmarket, ca.* 1717 (cat. no. 25), from the tapestry of *The Battle of Blenheim* hanging at Blenheim Palace among a series of battle scenes woven by de Vos for the Duke of Marlborough, *ca.* 1712.[39] In the 1761 sale of Wootton's collection there appeared "three sketches, the Battles of the Wood, and Blenheim, and Oudenarde,"[40] which seems to indicate that Wootton indeed visited Blenheim, for the battles of the Wood (Donauworth) and Oudenarde are represented there as well. This would also explain the points of contact between another tapestry in the series, *The Battle of Bouchain* (1) and one of Wootton's large sporting pictures in the hall at Althorp, *The View*, painted *ca.* 1730 for the 3rd Duke of Marlborough.[41] It is unlikely that either artist or patron was unaware of

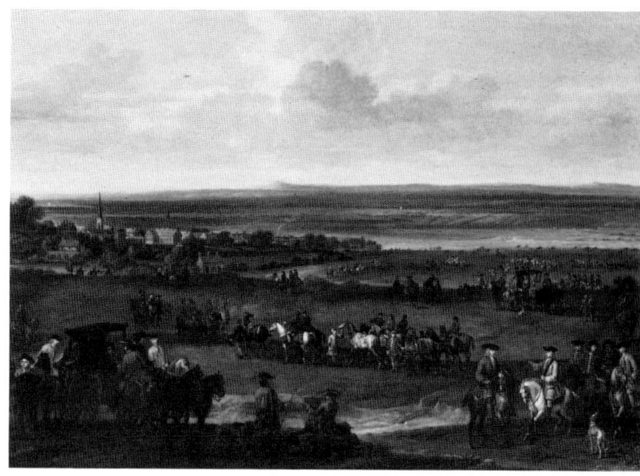

25. John Wootton: *George I at Newmarket, ca.* 1717

the military connotation assigned to sport by such borrowings.

Health, relaxation from work, nobility, and war were the most recurrent aspects of the sporting ideal in the eighteenth century, perhaps because they offered the most 'historical'—and thus weighty—defense to the increasing body of criticism. But sport was also celebrated on more modern grounds: it was said to promote social intercourse; to stimulate finer breeds of English horses (and so to be patriotic); and, not least, to be wholly justifiable merely because it was fun. These ideals saw wide expression in both print and paint.

We have already noted the theoretical connection between sport and the concept of nobility, but the more specific notion that sport encouraged social intercourse had a different basis. Written references to the delight of sport as a means of mixing socially with one's peers do not generally intend either to justify sport or to endow it with a special status; they merely reflect contemporary appreciation of one of the advantages it offered. Just as in modern times, prestigious race meetings were as much social events as sporting fixtures. "Races tolerable, the second ball very good" observed Mrs. Powys at Reading on August 25, 1794.[42] "Newmarket was charming; all the charming men were there,"[43] wrote the irrepressible Lady Sarah Lennox in 1763. Even Daniel Defoe, by no means a consistent friend of either sport or the fashionable rich, reported from Nottingham Races:

> I could give a long and agreeable Account of the Sport itself . . . but the illustrious Company . . . was in my Opinion, the Glory of the Day, for there we saw, besides eleven or twelve Noblemen, an infinite throng of Gentlemen from all the Countries around. Nor is the Appearance of the Ladies to be omitted . . . the Train of Coaches filled with the Beauties of the North, reminded me of the Garden of the Tuileries in Paris, or the Pardo at Mexico. . . .[44]

The gathering of illustrious figures at sporting events also provided the opportunity for more serious business than parade. Newmarket was a regular meeting ground for peers, a place where political plans might be made, campaigns launched, alliances forged.[45] Even local hunts could assume a political function, as at least one eighteenth-century writer argued:

> When the pleasures of the chase can be made the means of calling the gentlemen of the country together, they become really useful and beneficial to society. They give opportunities of wearing off shynesses, dispelling temporary differences, forming new friendships and cementing old, and draw the gentlemen of the country into one closer bond of society.[46]

While sporting pictures rarely should be thought to suggest directly any political connotation of a sporting event, there may often be found a firm stress on cameraderie, be it between members of a hunt or spectators at a race meeting. In Wootton's *George I at Newmarket, ca.* 1717 (cat. no. 25), the King is surrounded by refined and contented friends whose conversation, one might assume, is not necessarily related to the racehorses that parade behind their backs; the elegant ladies who sit in their carriage in the middle distance enjoy a day's outing in which horses are possibly not the main interest. In his *View of the Round Course at Newmarket, ca.* 1720 (cat. no. 45), Peter Tillemans gives the horse match that is about to begin no greater prominence than the groups of spectators and their activities. Some ladies and gentlemen anticipate the start of the race with eagerness, some admire each other. There is a sense of occasion to which the actual sport contributes only a part. Likewise, in a painting attributed to James Ross, *Racing at Newmarket, ca.* 1730,[47] a finely dressed group in the right foreground converses politely as the thrilling race, reaching its climax behind them, causes delight among their less distinguished cospectators.

In all these paintings one further issue becomes apparent. While sporting events may have acted as a meeting place for the wealthy, they also attracted the company of lower social classes. It has been suggested above that in certain sporting paintings the introduction of a peasant or tenant is designed to stress through contrast the status or nobility of the sportsman, but the mixing of social classes was a very real feature of race meetings, one which Wootton, Tillemans, and Ross portray faithfully. In the following century, when the ills of gambling were being discussed with some vigor, racing was argued in a House of Commons committee "to promote intercourse between different classes of society,"[48] but in earlier times the maintenance of rigid social distinctions was generally held to be essential. William Darrell advised his "Young Nobleman" to

> Converse not ordinarily with Persons above your Rank, nor with those that are below it; that will endanger your Estate, this your Breeding. . . . To herd with peasants is a Kind of voluntary Degradation . . . Peasantry is a Disease (like the Plague) easily caught by Conversation.[49]

Early- and mid-eighteenth-century pictures of race meetings seem to show little direct contact between upper and lower classes; they coexist, but rarely appear to be aware of each other. By the end of the century, when the chaos which attended races had become an issue of some concern, artists began to describe the inevitable, if haphazard, contact between classes—usually with some humor. William Mason's painting of *A Coun-*

try Race-course (etched by J. Jenkins and published by J. Philips, 1786)[50] shows peasants tumbling at the foot of a carriage occupied by an elegant, and distinctly alarmed, couple. Here at least the opportunity for the rich to mix with the poor at a race meeting is being politely refused.

Hunting too, it was eventually argued, promoted class unity. "It links all classes together from the Peer to the Peasant," wrote John Hawkes in 1808.[51] This ideal had not been forwarded specifically in the eighteenth century, when the exclusiveness of hunting was pressed strongly as one of its main attractions, but a local nobleman's theoretical role as guardian and benefactor in the community might allow him to claim that the spectacle provided by his sport furnished his wards with entertainment. In *Fox Hunting: Going Out*, 1800 (cat. no. 33), George Morland makes such contact between sportsman and peasant the subject of his picture, and in *Fox Hunting: Going to Cover*, 1801 (cat. no. 34), the notion of sport as spectacle—implied by the watching cottage dwellers in the background—is continued. Villagers, it has been suggested, liked hunting "for brightening their drab lives in bleak winter months,"[52] and in times of particular hardship their involvement, however peripheral, in their landlord's sport might well have raised morale. Were they themselves able to see pictures showing them enjoying their master's sport, their pleasure—and doubtless their loyalty—would be still greater. Thus it is of possible significance that in the 1730s—a period of severe agricultural depression[53]—John Wootton was commissioned to decorate the entrance halls of Althorp and Longleat with sporting scenes which show an unusual profusion of happy tenants.[54] Since entrance halls were traditionally a place where alms would be distributed to the poor and which acted, according to Isaac Ware, as "a reception place for servants . . . an ante-chamber in which people of business or the second rank wait and amuse themselves,"[55] Wootton's pictures may well have been intended by his patrons to entertain or even appease the needy tenants who undoubtedly would have seen them.[56]

Whatever the complexity of the sporting ideal and whatever the 'function' of a sporting picture might have been to its patron, the popularity of sporting art lay primarily in its capacity to entertain. Sport, for most of its practitioners, was a hobby; like most hobbies it provided entertainment through being undertaken both with a good deal of pleasure and with extreme seriousness. The most practical aspect of the latter to be given ideal expression was the notion that sport was a science. Technical sporting books were produced in profusion; by giving minute instruction in diverse sporting techniques and in the breeding and care of animals they attached to sport a scientific air which art helped to perpetuate. Indeed the beginnings of British sporting art were marked most clearly by Francis Barlow's illustrations to sporting books of the late seventeenth century. Barlow's drawings, etched by Hollar, for *Severall Wayes of Hunting, Hawking, and Fishing according to the English Manner*, 1671, and for Richard Blome's *The Gentleman's Recreation*, 1684, were intended in conjunction with the accompanying texts to educate the sportsman and to promote the idea that sport was as much a science as a recreation. Eighteenth-century sporting books frequently carried similar plates; Thomas Ross's drawing of *Netting Partridges* (cat. no. 38) is a careful explanation of technique which may originally have been intended as a design for one such illustration.

Eighteenth-century sporting paintings tended to be less didactic than this, but while on one level the wide demand for portraits of horses reflected patrons' simple pride of possession, the concern with the record of the appearance of a particular animal was equally a result of the preoccupation with breeding. Ever finer and ever faster strains of sporting horse were sought, found, raced, and painted. The Earl of Bath wrote in 1753, "The pedigree of these horses is more strictly regarded and carefully looked into than that of a Knight of Malta. . . . It is this care of the breed, and particularly with an eye to their strength, that makes all the world so fond of our horses."[57] The patriotic afterthought expressed a widely held view, although the English thoroughbred of course has oriental ancestry. During the seventeenth and eighteenth centuries nearly two hundred Arabian, Turkish, or Barbary steeds were imported into England in this search for perfection. Three of these—the Darley Arabian, the Byerly Turk, and the Godolphin Arabian—are the ancestors of the thoroughbred and as such were the subject of many sporting pictures commissioned both by owners and by admirers.[58] Paradoxically, the interest in the physical features peculiar to a particular horse or breed encouraged artistic distortions: long legs became longer or large Arabian eyes became larger in celebration of the notable aspects of a successful animal. Stubbs's portrait of *Eclipse* (cat. no. 44), however, probably included few such exaggerations. It becomes through its beauty and simplicity the painted equivalent of this artist's remarkable illustrations to the *Anatomy of the Horse*, 1766, a work in which Stubbs hoped "Gentlemen who breed horses will find advantage, as well as amusement, by acquiring an accurate knowledge of the structure of this beautiful and useful animal."[59]

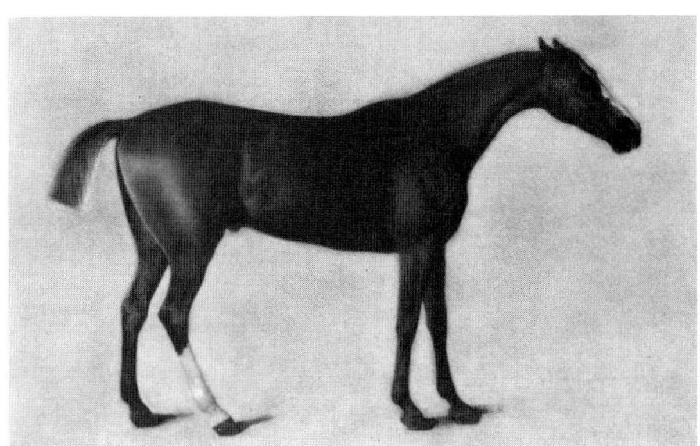

44. George Stubbs: *Eclipse* (detail), *ca.* 1770

The proof of the breeding is in the racing, and Eclipse—unbeaten in a career of twenty-six races and matches between 1769 and 1770—was the century's most successful racehorse. Sportsmen's scientific interest in breeding was naturally paralleled by their concern with a horse's achievements; this too is conveyed in certain sporting pictures. Richard Roper was commissioned to paint the scene at the finishing post in all three heats of the match between Aaron and Driver at Maidenhead in August 1754 (*Heat I*: cat. no. 37), and precise details of the progress of the races were even inscribed on the canvases. Likewise Wootton's *The Duke of Rutland's Bonny Black, ca.* 1715 (cat. no. 46), includes a painted scroll inscribed with a summary of the horse's racing career. In great contrast, however, to such serious aspects of the sportsman's attitude to his sport was the inclusion within the sporting ideal of considerably more jocular matter.

A popular eighteenth-century hunting song contained the following stanza:

> With sport, love and wine
> Fickle fortune defy;
> Dull wisdom all happiness sours:
> Since life is no more
> Than a passage at best,
> Let's strew the way over with flowers.[60]

This rather engaging recklessness was at the heart of the final constituent of the sporting ideal. The connections between sport, love, and wine were old in origin but were given particular prominence in the second half of the century. By popularizing the idea that sport was simply good fun they set the lighthearted tone which would pervade much sporting art of the nineteenth century. It does not require great imagination to understand the parallels which were drawn between the hunting of animals and the pursuit of women. The courtly frolics portrayed in the fifteenth-century "Devonshire" hunting tapestries (now in the Victoria & Albert Museum, London) provide evidence of the antiquity of this theme. Animals and maidens are chased in the same scenes; when a stag is caught a huntsman plunges his hand into its exposed entrails just as a nearby companion begins to ravish an unwilling female captive.[61] Hawking and courting were undertaken simultaneously by the dextrous in early seventeenth-century Flemish prints; spoils of the chase might be offered as homage to a woman in early eighteenth-century French art.[62] The tradition resumed in later eighteenth-century English art, made firmer by its popular expression in written form. The first issue of the *Sporting Magazine*, largely a manifesto containing justification for the foundation of such a journal, included a fictional letter which declared:

> I think I am too keen a sportsman. It is not the quadruped and winged game that are the objects of my attention. . . . I dare venture to attack the most-exalted animal of the chase—Woman is my mark![63]

The 'amorous sportsman' was a highly popular theme, and indeed was the subject and title of Francis Wheatley's painting of 1785, of which C. H. Hodges's mezzotint appears in this exhibition (cat. no. 66, ill. p. 20): a sportsman paws at an innocent girl while his dog does the same to already conquered game which lies at their side; a gun, the means by which game is won, is propped up nearby and has an obvious symbolic function.

"Let love crown the Night/And our sports crown the Day" ended one hunting song from an anthology which pointed out with frequency—and with varying degrees of politeness—how well a sportsman's activity by day was mirrored and complemented by his activity at night.[64] On such a level is the incident in Frederick George Byron's *Shooting Party Setting Out*, 1789 (cat. no. 29, ill. p. 20), in which the sportsman in the left background signals to the mildly flirtatious ladies in anticipation of 'game' he is soon to capture. In the companion piece, *Shooting Party Returning Home*, 1789 (cat. no. 30, ill. p. 20), this narrative is continued and is given greater pictorial prominence. On one level, of course, the sportsman's capture of game and its evident interest to the lady may be read in perfectly respectable terms: the man hunts; the woman cooks what is caught. But since in popular sporting mythology the hunt assumed a semisexual connotation, in this scene we are asked to imagine forthcoming activity other than cooking; the expression on the faces of the sportsman's companions suggest that they have begun to imagine already. In Marcellus Laroon's *Man and Woman with a Bag of Game* (cat. no. 58), the man's presentation of game and the carelessly dressed woman's acceptance of it

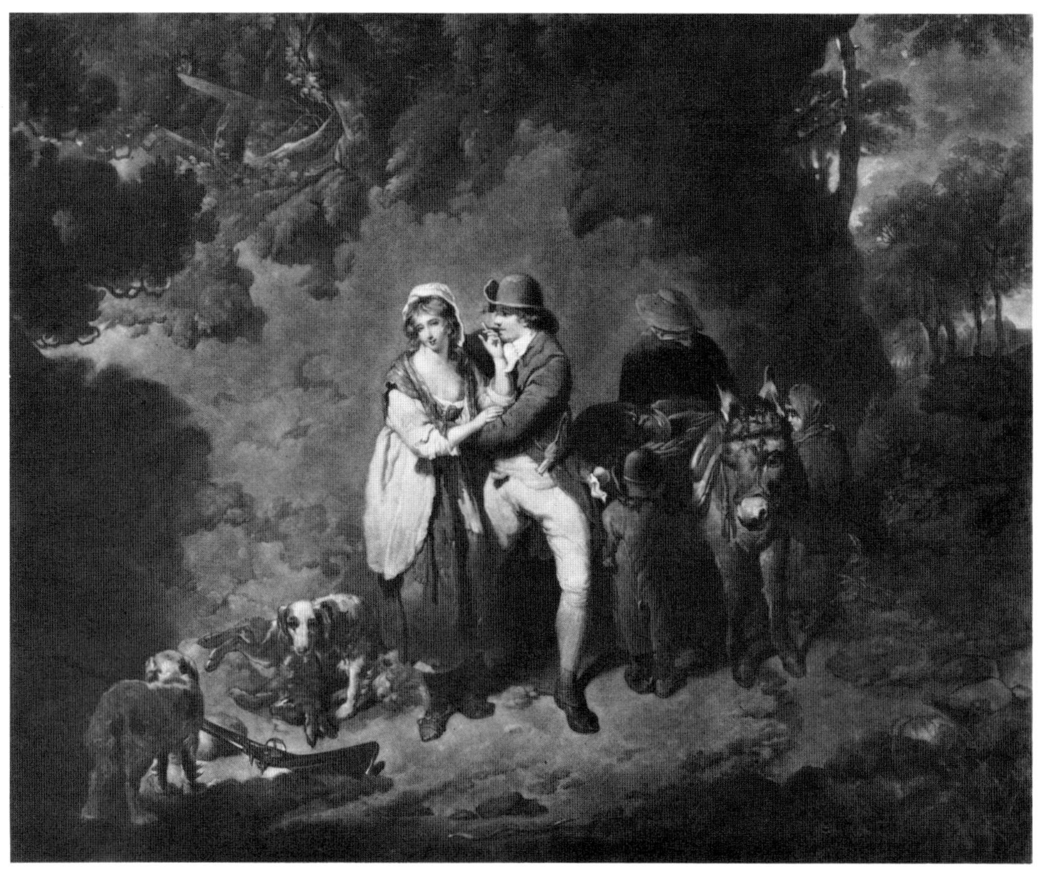

66. C. H. Hodges after Francis Wheatley: *The Amorous Sportsman*, 1786

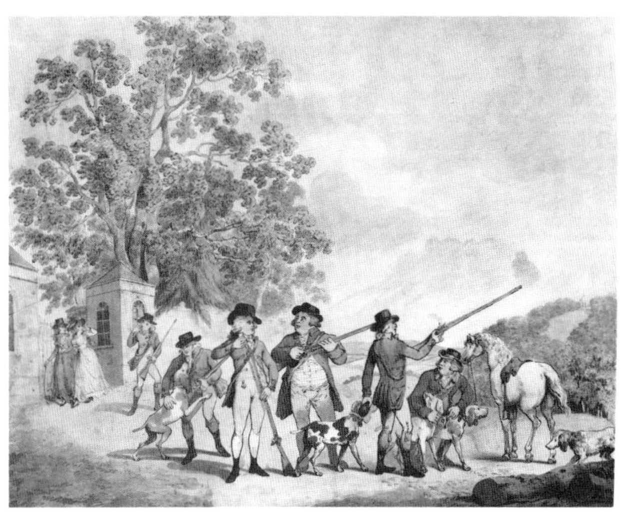

29. Frederick George Byron: *Shooting Party Setting Out*, 1789

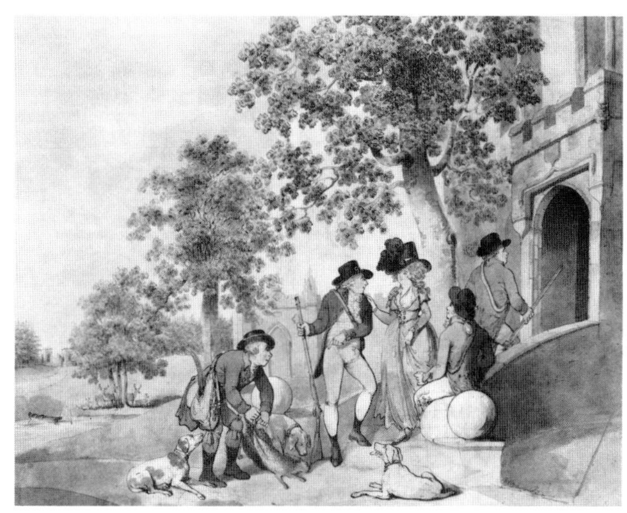

30. Frederick George Byron: *Shooting Party Returning Home*, 1789

carries a still more specific, and intentionally humorous, sexual implication which would have delighted an irreverent sporting spectator.

"May the smiles of the fair and the bottle reward the lovers of the Chase"[65] ran one eighteenth-century dinner toast, for sport and drinking also enjoyed a close popular connection which was emphasized particularly towards the end of the century when riotous fun became celebrated openly as an attraction of sport. Hunting songs stressed with wearisome persistence that a day of sport should be followed by a night of drunken festivity. An enthusiastic letter to the *Sporting Magazine* of November 1792 attempted to elevate the drinking ethic in a less than sober tone:

> Every sportsman is a lover of the bottle, provided it is not an empty one. I know not which is the most enchanting to behold, the much famed Diomed or the capacious honest quart, filled with the nectarious juice. The noble quadruped, indeed with his graceful symmetry and proportion, exhibits the standard of perfection in that generous race of animals; but look at the alluring bottle! how stately! how erect! and how delicious are its contents!

The revelling sportsmen in Rowlandson's *The Dinner*, 1787 (cat. no. 63), are similarly boisterous and drawn with similar humor; it is worth noting that the artist places a large sporting painting on the wall to remind them of the activity which is the ostensible cause of their merriment. Such scenes would have added fuel to the

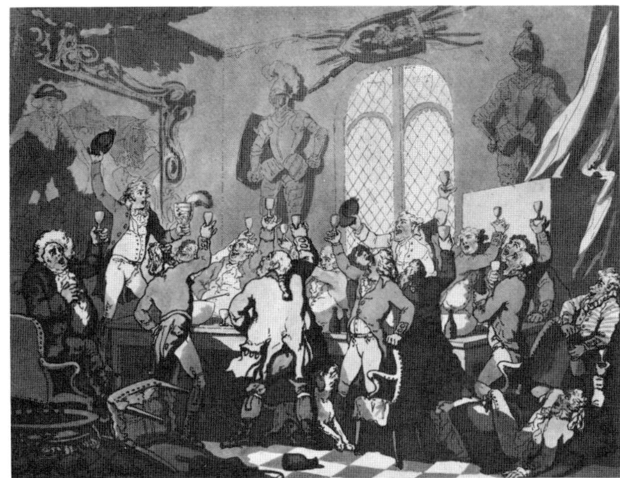

63. Thomas Rowlandson: *The Dinner*, 1787

moral fire of those critics of sport whose arguments will be discussed shortly, but they were popular among sportsmen as expressions of this final, and very tangible, aspect of the sporting ideal.

The sporting ideal was thus both multifaceted and susceptible to changes in emphasis as the century progressed. The new and less grave body of sporting culture which gained ground in the later years did not, however, begin to supersede the more traditional ideology until the following century. This coexistence of old and new ideals contributed much to the unique variety in the pictorial celebration of eighteenth-century rural sport.

Notes

1. *An Essay on Hunting*, p. 12.

2. Sir Thomas Elyot, *The Book named The Governor*, ed. S. E. Lehmberg (New York and London, 1962), p. xvi.

3. Henry Peacham, *The Compleat Gentleman* (1622), ed. G. S. Gordon (Oxford, 1906), p. 216.

4. J. Armstrong, *The Art of Preserving Health* (London, 1744), p. 5.

5. John Careless, *The Old English Squire* (London, 1821), p. 43.

6. From verses captioning William Woollett's line engraving, published by Thomas Bradford, 1 August 1769, after Stubbs's *Two Gentlemen going a shooting, with a view of Creswell Crags: taken on the spot*. Judy Egerton has suggested to me in correspondence that one of the two sportsmen portrayed in the *Shooting* scenes may be Mr. William Wildman (an early patron of Stubbs), who died in 1784. In the sale of his collection of pictures (Christie's, Jan. 19–20 1787), among 14 paintings by Stubbs were lot 85, "A pair of shooting pieces," sold for £48.16.6., and lot 86, "Ditto," sold for the same amount. Mrs. Egerton suggests that these were the four *Shooting* scenes now at the BAC, and that there is a reasonable likeness between the appearance of the man in the dark tunic in this series and the Mr. Wildman portrayed in Stubbs's *Eclipse with William Wildman and his two Sons* (Baltimore Museum of Art). The high prices of the 4 pictures in the sale, which took place during Stubbs's lifetime, suggest that they were not copies; unless, therefore, they were second versions by Stubbs himself (and none are known of these subjects) they are very likely to be the 4 that are now at the BAC. Unfortunately, even if Mr. Wildman once owned them, Stubbs's inconsistencies in his portraiture of the 2 gentlemen through the series make difficult a positive identification of either of them on the basis of comparisons with other portraits. However, since the appearance of the Mr. Wildman in the Baltimore picture is no *less* like that of the dark-clothed man in *Shooting* (1) than is the appearance of the same man in, for example, *Shooting* (4), the implication of the documentary evidence cannot be discounted on visual grounds, and a tentative identification may indeed be made. I am extremely grateful to Mrs. Egerton for bringing this to my attention.

7. Quoted in *Sports and Pastimes in English Literature*, ed. L. S. Wood and H. L. Burrows (London, 1925), p. 112.

8. From *A New Hunting Song* in *The Royal Sportsman's Delight* (London, 1765).

9. See, for example, Michael Levey, *Rococo to Revolution* (London, 1966).

10. *The Sportsman's Dictionary: or the Country Gentleman's Companion in all Rural Recreations*, vol. 1 (London, 1735), p. 1.

11. *The Complete Family-Piece* (London, 1737), preface, p. vii.

12. *Policratus*, p. 18.

13. Richard Brathwait, *The English Gentleman* (London, 1643), pp. 165, 174.

14. The Earl of Chesterfield, *Letters to his son* (London, 1827), vol. 2, p. 3 (1749).

15. *An Essay on Hunting*, p. 23.

16. *The Spectator*, no. 115.

17. See Roy Strong, *Charles I on Horseback* (Harmondsworth, 1972), p. 49.

18. Peacham, *Compleat Gentleman*, p. 217.

19. Daniel Defoe, *A Tour Through England and Wales* (1724–26), vol. 1 (New York, 1959), p. 76.

20. *The World*, I, no. 17 (1753).

21. Reproduced in Walker, *Sporting Art*, pl. 55.

22. Daniel Defoe, *The True Born Englishman*, ed. Sir Walter Scott (London, 1888), p. 442.

23. A foreground beggar or peasant is a motif which appears frequently in Wootton's work. See *Lord Portmore Watching Racehorses at Exercise* (cat. no. 48).

24. William Somerville, *The Chace* (London, 1735), bk. 1.

25. *An Essay on Hunting*, p. 19.

26. *The Gentleman's Magazine*, March 1734, pp. 154–55.

27. Butcher's *Survey and Antiquity of the Towne of Stamford*, 1646.

28. *Hounslow Heath, a poem* (by Welthenhall Wilkes?) (London, 1747).

29. P. 49.

30. *An Essay on Hunting*, pp. 7, 27.

31. See *An Estimate of the Manners and Principles of the Times*, J. Brown (London, 1757), passim.

32. Peacham, *Compleat Gentleman*, p. 217.

33. *The Works of the English Poets from Chaucer to Cowper*, ed. Samuel Johnson and A. Chalmers (London, 1810), vol. 2, p. 152.

34. Somerville, *The Chace*, bk. 4.

35. See *Memoir of Thomas Bewick—written by himself*, ed. Edmund Blunden (London, 1961), p. 189.

36. See Aubrey Noakes, *Sportsmen in a Landscape* (London, 1954), p. 205.

37. *The Sportsman's Evening Brush* (London, 1792), p. 87.

38. Judy Egerton, *British Sporting and Animal Paintings*, p. 6.

39. Ibid., p. 15.

40. I would like to thank Judy Egerton for bringing this to my attention. See *A Catalogue of the collection of Pictures of Mr. J. Wootton* (London, 1761), British Museum, C. 119.h.3 (53).

41. The tapestries are reproduced in Alan Wace, *The Marlborough Tapestries at Blenheim Palace* (London and New York, 1968). *The View* is reproduced in Sparrow, *British Sporting Artists*, pp. 104–05. There are also similarities in both detail and conception between the Blenheim battle tapestries and the hunting tapestries at Clandon Park, Surrey, woven after designs by Wootton *ca.* 1740.

42. *Passages from the Diaries of Mrs. Lybbe Powys of Hardwick House, Oxon AD 1756–1808*, ed. E. J. Climenson (London, 1899), p. 278.

43. Quoted in Sir Theodore Cook, *Character and Sportsmanship* (London, 1927), p. 61.

44. Defoe, *A Tour Through England*, vol. 2, p. 148.

45. See Mingay, *English Landed Society*, pp. 150–51.

46. Sir Christopher Sykes to T. Grimston, 5 Dec. 1792, quoted in David C. Itzkowitz, *Peculiar Privilege* (Sussex, 1977), p. 19.

47. *Annual Exhibition of Sporting Paintings*, 1976, Richard Green, no. 4.

48. *Horse Racing: Its History* (London, 1865), p. 12.

49. William Darrell, *A Gentleman Instructed in the Conduct of a Virtuous and Happy Life* (London, 1704), pp. 28–29.

50. Reproduced in *British Sporting Painting 1650–1850* (Arts Council exhibition catalogue, 1974), p. 134.

51. Quoted in Itzkowitz, *Peculiar Privilege*, p. 25.

52. E. W. Bovill, *English Country Life 1780–1830* (Oxford, 1962), p. 206.

53. See G. E. Mingay, "The Agricultural Depression 1730–5," *Economic History Review*, 2nd series, VIII, (1955).

54. Some of the Althorp and Longleat paintings are reproduced in *Country Life* (1958), pp. 1292–93. For Longleat, see also *Country Life* (1949), p. 928. Engravings after the Longleat series are included in the Mellon Collection (Dudley Snelgrove, *English Sporting and Animal Prints 1658–1874*, p. 210).

55. Isaac Ware, quoted in J. Fowler and J. Cornforth, *English Decoration in the Eighteenth Century* (London, 1974), p. 241.

56. For an adventurous discussion of the attitudes of the rich towards the poor and their effect on English art, see J. Barrell, *The Dark Side of the Landscape: The Rural Poor in English Painting 1730–1840* (Cambridge, 1980).

57. *The World*, I, no. 17.

58. See Walker, *Sporting Art*, pp. 58–59.

59. George Stubbs, *Anatomy of the Horse* (London, 1766), preface.

60. *Nimrod's Songs of the Chase* (London, 1788), p. 14.

61. See pl. 31 in G. W. Digby, *The Devonshire Hunting Tapestries* (London, 1971).

62. See figs. 108, 143 in W. A. Baillie-Grohman, *Sport in Art from the Fifteenth to the Eighteenth Century* (London, 1913).

63. The *Sporting Magazine*, I (October, 1792), p. 20.

64. From *The Sweet Rosy Morning* in *The Delights of the Chace* (London, *ca.* 1780).

65. *The Sportsman's Evening Brush*, p. 87.

II. *The Criticism of Sport*

> Take care how you meddle with Country Squires: They are the Ornaments of the English Nation; Men of Good Heads and sound Bodies! and let me tell you, some of them take it ill of you, that you mention Fox-hunters with so little Respect.
>
> "Sir Roger de Coverley" to "Mr. Spectator," *The Spectator*, no. 34, April 1711

The expression of a sporting ideal in eighteenth-century art and literature may be seen both as a response and a stimulus to the critics of sport. Pictures and books which extolled the traditional virtues of a sporting life were popular among sportsmen partly because they bolstered the apparent worth of an activity which was being subjected to systematic criticism; those which publicized the more modern aspects of the ideal must also have helped—usually without intention—to encourage further criticism. This interrelationship of the ideal and its opposition is of some importance. While it would be a difficult task to measure precisely how far the 'publicity' provided by deliberately favorable written and visual representations of sport ultimately provoked disapproval, an understanding of the various grounds of the criticism may help to explain why idealization was popular or necessary in the first place.

The eighteenth century has been characterized as an age in which pleasure and happiness were pursued with unusual enthusiasm and success.[1] If such a generalization is to be made, the concurrent and increasingly moralistic concern with manners and with standards of behavior in all levels of society should also be noted. Steele and Addison's writings in the *Tatler* and *Spectator* early in the century promoted with wit and subtlety the idea of the "well-bred gentleman." In so doing, they formalized standards of correct behavior and began what has been described as a "cultural revolution."[2] This was perhaps more a revolution in attitude than in reality. Excess among the aristocracy may have been "*regarded* as a bad example to the lower orders," as G. E. Mingay has argued,[3] but as far as sport was concerned moderation among the upper classes was notable by its absence throughout the century. It thus provided those with a concern for England's moral welfare with an obvious target for criticism.

The apparent excess with which sport was undertaken was argued first to be an evil in itself. In 1704 William Darrell constructed a code of behavior for "A Young Nobleman" which did not allow the practice of rural sports. "I blame not the Recreation, but the Excess,"[4] he explained, drawing on a theme expressed with charm seventy years earlier by Richard Brathwait: "If wee eat too much honey, it will grow distastfull, so in recreations, if we exceed, they must needs grow hurtfull."[5] It is quite clear from the written evidence of sportsmen themselves that such warnings were largely ignored in the eighteenth century. Writing to the Duke of Richmond to decline an invitation to hunt at Goodwood, William Pulteney (later Earl of Bath) noted, "I am not yet well enough established in my health to do it. Temperance and regularity are still necessary for me to observe, and at Goodwood I believe no-one ever heard of either of them."[6] A certain sense of pride in their lack of moderation was not uncommon among sportsmen. Colonel Thornton, a famous sporting figure at the turn of the century (and a patron of Sawrey Gilpin and George Garrard), took pleasure in releasing to the press in 1803 details of his forthcoming sporting program at Thornville Royal:

> On Monday, stag-hunting, followed by coursing; Tuesday, wolf, stag and fox hunting, and beagling; Wednesday, stag-hunting and coursing; Thursday, wolf, stag, and fox hunting, beagling and coursing.[7]

In others, such tendencies towards excess were considerably less conscious, but doubtless quite as disturbing to proponents of proper behavior; Nicholas Blundell's matter-of-fact diary entry for 24 September 1704 reads, "My Wife felt ye Pains of Labour coming upon her. Captain Fazackerley and I went a coursing."[8]

Bankruptcy among the upper classes, idleness among the lower classes, and moral degradation for both were commonly held to be the specific products of excess in sport. Financial acumen was considered to be a necessary quality in a successful landowner, for while the majority of the old aristocracy was reasonably secure in its wealth at least until the end of the century, the loss or reduction of estates among any landed class was not infrequent.[9] Extravagance was a luxury few could afford. Horse racing was of course a particularly expensive activity, one which, as Robert Burton had stressed in the previous century, could lead men "to gallop quite out of their fortunes."[10] The trend became more prevalent in reality with the expansion of sport. The Duke of Kingston, for example, had been warned as a boy by his tutor that "Play is the only thing that can well ruin a Great Estate." He went on to pursue with enthusiasm a career at Newmarket at an estimated cost of £7000 per annum; severe financial crises in 1779 and 1795 were solved only by selling considerable portions of land.[11] Similarly, Richard Grosvenor began his adult life as one of the richest men in England, spent at least £300,000 on hunting and racing, and died in 1802 with debts of over £100,000.[12] The criticism of sport on the grounds of its excessive expense was neither difficult to prove nor rare.

Racing was thought by some to be damaging to others besides the upper classes. *An Act to restrain and prevent the excessive Increase of Horse Races* was passed during the reign of George II to raise the minimum prize money permissible at race meetings, because, the preamble argued, "small prizes or sums of money had contributed very much to the encouragement of idleness, to the impoverishment of many of the meaner sort of subjects of this Kingdom."[13] Gambling lay at the heart of the popularity of horse racing for spectators and was its most widely criticized vice. An act during the reign of Queen Anne, addressed to "divers persons (lewd and dissolute),"[14] had, in fact, attempted to curtail the spread of gambling, but with predictably little success. Gambling offered the rich the chance to become richer, and the poor the chance to become less poor; or, as one contemporary writer put it: "it stimulates the insatiate appetite of one, and holds out strong allurements to the other."[15] *The Gentleman's Magazine* in September 1743 objected to racing on the grounds that gambling lured the lower classes away from their jobs; *Newmarket, or an Essay on the Turf* noted that its natural consequence was "quarrelling and duels."[16] In short, gambling was seen to be both socially damaging and unseemly. Moreover it encouraged the nobility to demean themselves and gave lesser men the opportunity to infiltrate the ranks of their social superiors. The Duke of Bedford, it was suggested, saw the Turf not merely as an amusement but "reduced himself to a level with the lowest blackleg, by scandalous zeal to convert it into profit";[17] meanwhile the acquisition of money through gambling allowed other men to be "elected into a society, where formerly none but persons of real rank and character were admitted."[18] One further example may be cited of the view that the lure of profit and the mixing of classes that it encouraged combined to provide a threat to both the moral tone of society and the maintenance of class distinctions. An anonymous poet wrote in 1735:

> On Epsom Downs when Racing does begin
> Large companies from every part come in,
> Tag-rag and Bob-tail, Lords and Ladies meet,
> And Squires without Estates each other greet;
> A Scoundrel here, pray take it on my word,
> Is a companion for the greatest Lord
> Provided that his purse abounds with gold
> —If not, then this affection will not hold.[19]

Equally offensive to commentators upon public morality was the apparent connection between sport and drinking. By the end of the century, as we have seen, sportsmen were openly advertising drinking as an enjoyable accompaniment to their pastime; the suggestion that it was healthy fun was perhaps the only possible answer to moralists who had been criticizing the connection since the previous century. Because sport and drinking were both recreations which often accompanied each other in reality and which both became impolite in excess, critics of one tended to mention the other almost automatically. In 1671 John Evelyn noted with disapproval at Newmarket "the jolly blades racing, dancing, feasting, and revelling, more resembling a luxurious and abandoned rout than a Christian Court."[20] The revelry that often accompanied sport thus came to discredit sport itself, thereby explaining Lord Chesterfield's otherwise curious grouping of "sottish drinking, indiscriminate gluttony, driving coaches, [and] rustic sports" to comprise his list of "pleasures that degrade a gentleman."[21] For the lower classes, the festival atmosphere of race meetings naturally encouraged enthusiastic drinking, strengthening the belief of those who thought that England was suffering from "scenes of misery, folly, and vice, which would never be witnessed among us but for the races."[22] Whether or not this conclusion was fairly drawn, it is certainly true that the drinking bouts of Thomas Turner, an eighteenth-century shopkeeper and diarist, often coincided with his attendance at sporting events. In August 1758, for example, after a visit to Lewes races he recorded "I came in in company with Mr. Francis Elliss, about ten; but, to my shame do I say it, very much in liquor."[23]

Such morally suspect aspects of sport were simple to criticize because they appeared to have a firm factual base, and as the century progressed gambling, drinking, and excessive indulgence in sport undoubtedly increased in reality as much as in discussion. With a possibly less firm base was the very popular notion that sportsmen in general were unlearned and tedious people. Since sport was widely associated with excess it became fashionable to suggest that its practitioners were capable of thinking of little else. In 1704 William Darrell expressed a view which was to become increasingly common among nonsportsmen:

> Good God! how often have I lost Patience, and fretted away good Humour in the Company of Gentlemen of four Estates, and of noble Extraction, methought they had serv'd an Apprenticeship under Grooms or Dog-Boys; they eternally grated my Ears with Hounds and Horses, and broke out into such clamorous Tumults, as if they had been drawing up the Grievances of the Nation, or pelting the Prerogative; yet after all, the Question was only, whether Puss or Lightfoot got the better last Chace. Racing and Hunting are indeed laudable Recreations; and upon Occasions may be discourst of; but then to harp perpetually upon these Creatures, is an infallible Argument their Thoughts are mean, and too weak wing'd to soar above the Beast.[24]

This attitude was the basis of many jokes in *The Spectator* at the expense of sportsmen. Addison's invention of Sir Roger de Coverley—a bluff, no-nonsense, and somewhat simple country gentleman with a passion for sport—helped to perpetuate the idea that sport was in opposition to learning, and influenced William Shenstone's rather unkind mid-century declaration that "the world may be divided into people that read, people that write, people that think, and fox hunters."[25]

In such a climate of opinion it is hardly surprising that the idealization of sport in art and literature should be of some importance to sportsmen. Whether objections to sport were made in moral terms or simply used as a vehicle for humor they were considered by some to be offensive, and it was not uncommon for sporting writers to express the hope that their discussion of the benefits of sport might help to correct certain popular misconceptions.[26] If the sporting ideal was thus in one sense a means of defense, sporting art may be seen as part of the bulwark. Artists whose work encouraged the association of sport with virtuous qualities inevitably helped their patrons in the search for respect. And, in the same way that to buy or commission any painting announced a gentleman's intellectual capacity, to hang a painting of sport on the wall was to attempt to elevate publicly the status of his pastime.

Paintings, prints, or drawings which drew attention to the less virtuous side of sport were influenced by the written criticisms, but were not necessarily unpopular among sportsmen if their message was sufficiently ambiguous. John Nixon's *Brighton Races*, 1805 (cat. no. 59), is a humorous summary of incidents that might occur at a race meeting. We see fun but also chaos, fine coaches and bolting horses, lords and beggars, coquettes

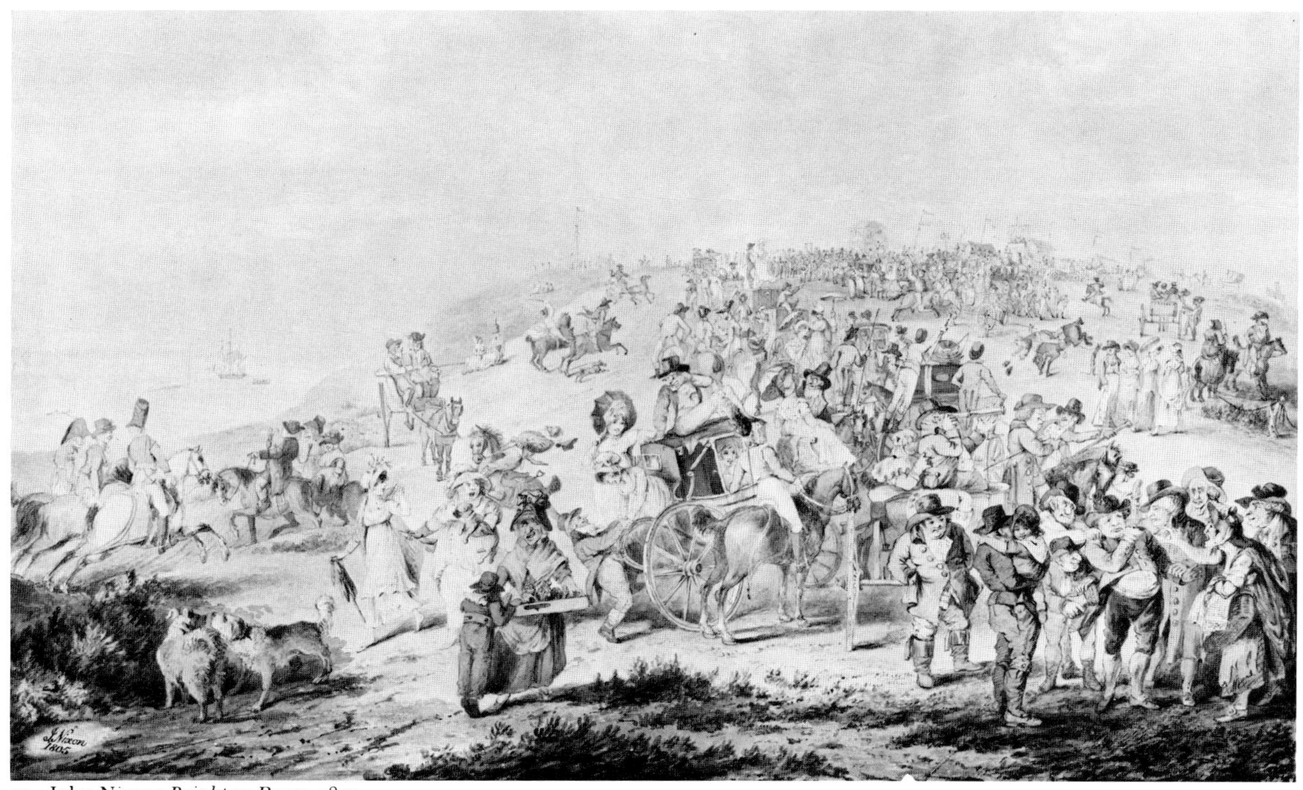

59. John Nixon: *Brighton Races*, 1805

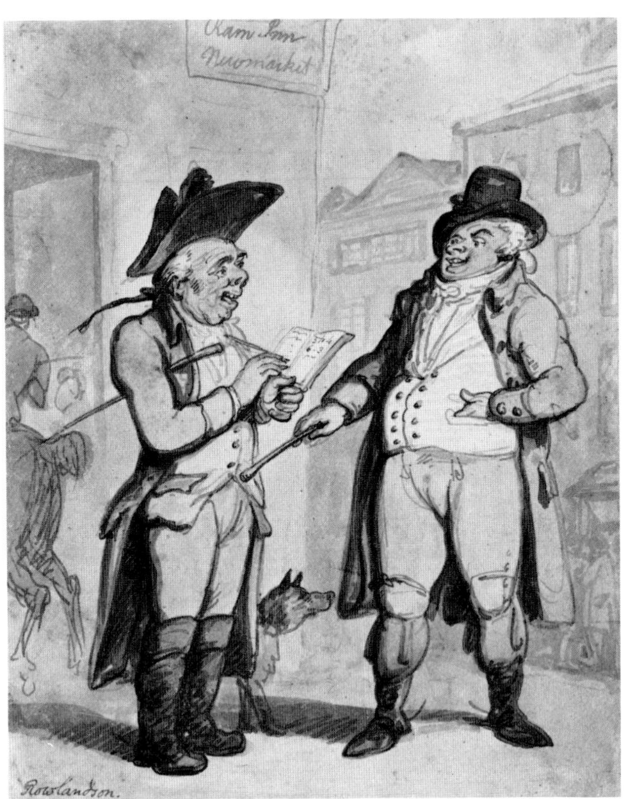

60. Thomas Rowlandson: *Bookmaker and Client Outside The Ram Inn, Newmarket*

and lechers. A horse match in progress may well be implied, out of view to the right, but it is of little apparent interest to the majority of the crowd, whose variety and activity is the intended subject of the picture. To critics of sport this scene would provide 'proof' of the moral laxity which was said to attend the races, and might itself influence future critics. For sportsmen, on the other hand, it immortalized the modern aspect of the sporting ideal by showing sport as a social occasion in which enjoyment—be it of the horses or of the opposite sex—needed no justification. Similar comments may be applied to Rowlandson's *Epsom in 1804*.[27] People of all social classes are grouped at the finishing post. Some watch the race and show glee or dismay at the imminent outcome; others, women drinking and soldiers groping, make merry on the grass. It is a scene of unbridled pleasure that explains both contemporary criticism and celebration of sport.

Most humorous representations of sport have this dual nature; indeed the uncompromising and severe written criticisms barely seem to have a parallel in eighteenth-century British art. Painters of sport were patronized almost exclusively by sportsmen, and so we may assume that their freedom of expression was understandably limited. But caricaturists who gently ridiculed sport were thought harmless at worst, and, since jollity had become part of the sporting ideal, were actually appreciated by sportsmen. Henry William Bunbury's *Patience in a Punt* (cat. no. 51) seems to suggest that fishing is incurably boring, but it is drawn with a humor that would offend few. Even his *Sporting Undergraduate*, 1772 (cat. no. 50), which shows a choice between learning and sport being decided in favor of the latter—the precise equivalent of the written opinions quoted above on the ignorance of sportsmen—is not malicious. Rowlandson's *Bookmaker and Client Outside The Ram Inn, Newmarket* (cat. no. 60) is possibly a little more severe, for in showing both parties pleased with a transaction by which one of them will ultimately lose, the artist makes a wry and almost moralistic comment on gambling. But even here there is room for an alternative interpretation, for it may be argued that gambling is shown to be an enjoyable game of chance which brings smiles to its practitioners.

The issue of cruelty to animals is of course at the forefront of modern arguments against rural sport, but it was not until the late eighteenth century that objections on this basis were voiced with any consistency.[28] Cruelty to domestic animals was widely discussed from the 1770s onwards, but a typical early work of this kind, the Rev. James Granger's *An Apology for the Brute Creation or the Abuse of Animals Censured*, 1772, made little mention of hunting—and then only to express concern for

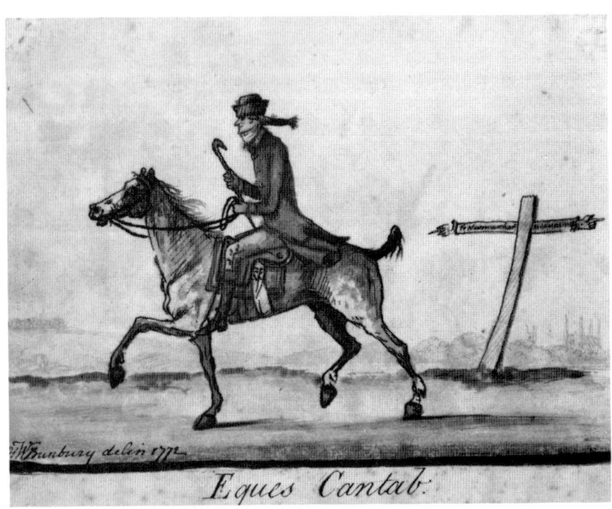

50. Henry William Bunbury, *The Sporting Undergraduate*, 1772

the welfare of the horses and hounds that did the chasing. After all, sportsmen could argue convincingly that birds and hares were hunted because they were food, foxes because they were vermin, and stags very rarely anyway. However in 1776 another religious tract, Humphry Primatt's *Dissertation on the Duty of Mercy and the Sin of Cruelty to Brute Animals*, specifically denounced hunting on the grounds that the infliction of pain upon hunted animals was morally indefensible, and from the 1780s this theme was to recur with frequency. William Cowper wrote in 1783 of

> . . . Detested Sport
> That owes its pleasure to another's pain;
> That feeds upon the sobs and dying shrieks
> of harmless nature.[29]

And Dr. Hawksworth, in an essay accompanying Thomas Gooch's *Life and Death of a Race Horse*, 1792, added

> There is a great difference between killing for food, and for sport. To take pleasure in that by which pain is inflicted, if it is not vicious, is dangerous; and every practice which if not criminal in itself, yet wears out the sympathizing sensibility of a tender mind, must render human nature proportionally less fit for society.[30]

As common as this moral or sociological angle was a more sentimental approach. It has been pointed out recently that late eighteenth-century opponents of cruelty in hunting expressed little sympathy for the 'wily fox'—"a beast of prey, greedy of blood, a robber prowling about"[31]—but much for the 'timid hare,' which was defended in children's stories such as *The Hare, or Hunting Incompatible with Humanity*, 1799, or *Sandford and Merton*, 1783–89. Earlier in the century, in Henry Fielding's *Joseph Andrews* a tearful Fanny had objected to "the barbarity of worrying a poor innocent defenceless animal out of its life, and putting it to the extremest torture for diversion" but was unable to "prevail on Joseph, who had been a sportsman in his youth, to attempt anything contrary to the laws of hunting in favour of the hare, which he said was killed fairly."[32] By the 1790s, however, it had become distinctly unfashionable for sportsmen to show any delight at the death of defenseless hares. Pictorial representations of the death of wily foxes were always popular. In Morland's *Fox Hunting: The Death*, 1800 (cat. no. 35), the huntsmen gloat as the prey is caught and killed; only a woman, naturally squeamish we must suppose, expresses dismay from her cottage window. But the explicit depiction of *hares* dying at the end of hunts became increasingly rare in British art in the last years of the century. Indeed Sawrey Gilpin's *A Young Man with Horse, Hounds,*

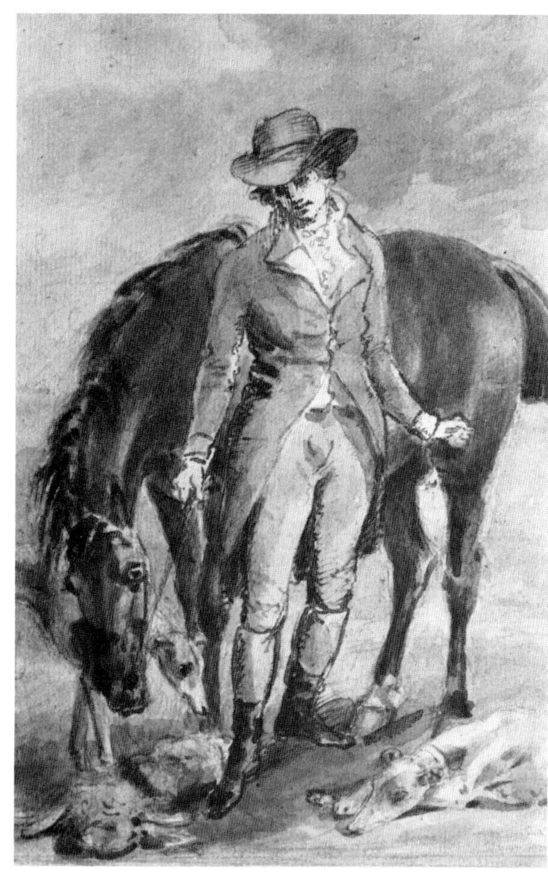

71. Sawrey Gilpin: *A Young Man with Horse, Hounds, and Dead Hare, ca.* 1795

and Dead Hare, ca. 1795 (cat. no. 71), shows a huntsman looking at the hare he has killed with sympathy and even regret; his horse and hounds, meanwhile, show similar dejection. It is an early example of a rare species, the antihunting picture, and, significantly, it is a drawing rather than a commissioned painting.

Gilpin's drawing holds little of the ambiguity, noted above, which was usually present in pictures that describe the less wholesome aspects of sport. In this respect, George Stubbs's *Freeman, the Earl of Clarendon's Gamekeeper, with a Dying Doe and a Hound*, 1800 (cat. no. 73, ill. p. 28), is more conventional: commissioned at a time when cruelty in sport had become an issue of public interest, this painting may be seen either as a defense or as a criticism of blood sports. Since its patron, Thomas Villiers, 2nd Lord Clarendon, was a keen sportsman, we may assume his attitude matched that assigned by Stubbs to the gamekeeper: Freeman shows not a trace of remorse at having shot the doe and defiantly looks at the spectator as he prepares to slit the animal's throat with a knife; the game has been successfully and fairly won. But at the same time the artist invites us to sympathize with the doe, which turns to appeal to the viewer as does the hound to its master. Just as Gilpin's horse and hound sympathize with their dead fellow creature, Stubbs's hound is linked pictorially and emotionally with the doe. The doe pleads to us for its life; the hound pleads to Freeman; Freeman prepares to defy everyone. The picture may be read at many levels but nothing is more certain than its ambiguity. While Stubbs's own regard for animals of all kinds is likely to have involved an opposition to their wanton killing, as a painter of sport he relied largely on sportsmen for patronage. It is hardly surprising that he did not openly join the critics of sport whose arguments, as we have seen, had gathered considerable force in the eighteenth century.

Pictures which touched upon so sensitive a subject as cruelty were part of a wider movement towards the end of the century within which certain artists attempted to extend the range of their subject matter beyond the confines of earlier patronage. The criticism of sport, therefore, which originally catalyzed the expression of a sporting ideal, eventually provided artists with one means of reducing their dependence on an ideal generated by sporting society alone.

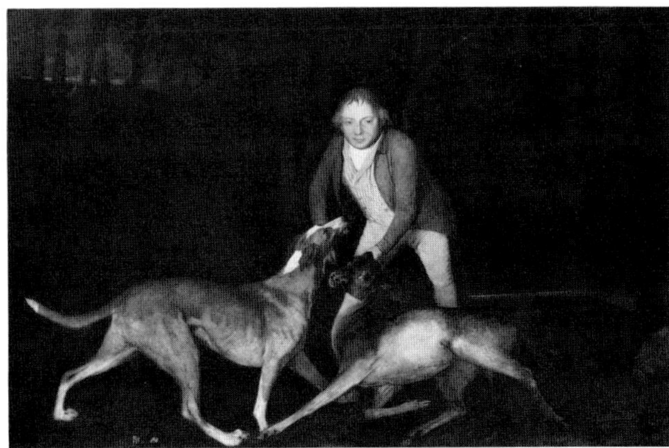

73. George Stubbs: *Freeman, the Earl of Clarendon's Gamekeeper, with a Dying Doe and a Hound* (detail), 1800

Notes

1. See Plumb, *The Pursuit of Happiness*, passim.
2. See Mingay, *English Landed Society*, p. 146.
3. Ibid., p. 145.
4. Darrell, *A Gentleman Instructed*, p. 36.
5. Brathwait, *The English Gentleman*, p. 171.
6. Quoted in David Hunn, *Goodwood* (London, 1975), p. 48.
7. Quoted in Noakes, *Sportsmen in a Landscape*, p. 204.
8. *Blundell's Diary and Letter Book 1702–1728*, ed. M. Blundell (Liverpool, 1952).
9. See Williams, *Life in Georgian England*, chaps. 2, 3.
10. Robert Burton, *Anatomy of Melancholy* (London, 1660), chap. 4, sec. 2, p. 2.
11. Mingay, *English Landed Society*, p. 151.
12. See Judy Egerton, "The Painter and the Peer," *Country Life* (1979), pp. 1892–93.
13. 13 Geo. II Cap. 19.
14. 9th Anne Cap. 14.
15. *The Minor Jockey Club* (London, 1792), p. ii.
16. *Newmarket, or an Essay on the Turf*, p. 43.
17. *The Jockey Club* (London, 1792), p. 17.
18. *The Minor Jockey Club*, p. ii.
19. Quoted in Wood and Burrows, *Sports and Pastimes*, p. 97.
20. John Evelyn, *The Diary of John Evelyn*, ed. W. Bray (London, 1895), Oct. 1671.
21. The Earl of Chesterfield, *Letters . . . to his son*, published by Mrs. Eugenia Stanhope (London, 1827), vol. 2, p. 3.
22. Rev. Francis Close, *The Evil Consequences of attending the Race Course exposed in a Sermon* (London and Cheltenham, 1827).
23. *The Diary of Thomas Turner . . . 1754–1765*, ed. Florence Maris Turner (London, 1925), p. 42.
24. Darrell, *A Gentleman Instructed*, p. 25.
25. Esmé Wingfield-Stratford, *The Squire and his Relations* (London, 1956), p. 187.
26. See, for example, John Lawrence, *A Philosophical and Practical Treatise on Horses* (London, 1796–98), vol. 2, p. 15.
27. Reproduced in Noakes, *Sportsmen in a Landscape*, opposite p. 212.
28. James Thomson's discussion in *The Seasons: Autumn*, 1730, of "this falsely cheerful, barbarous game of death" (line 384) is an early published example of antihunting sentiment paying particular attention to animals' suffering. Bruce Robertson has brought to my attention a reference to a possibly earlier description of hunting as "detestable . . . tragical . . . inhuman," cited in a letter from the Earl of Cardigan to the Duke of Montague, *ca.* 1750. See *Historical Manuscripts Commission: Report of Duke of Buccleuch and Queensberry*, vol. 1 (1899).
29. *The Task* (1784), book 3: "The Garden," ll. 326–29.
30. The essay "Tending to excite a Benevolent Conduct towards the Brute Creation, by the late Dr. Hawksworth" appeared at the end of Gooch's book of plates.
31. The quotation is from Lawrence, *Treatise on Horses*, vol. 2, p. 14, and is cited in Itzkowitz, *Peculiar Privilege*, p. 140, in a useful discussion of the anticruelty movement. Note that Thomson's *Autumn* had declared "Poor is the triumph o'er the timid hare" (l. 401).
32. Henry Fielding, *Joseph Andrews*, ed. George Sainsbury (London and New York, 1910), pp. 183–84.

III. Restrictions and Reactions

'Tis said that naught so much the temper rubs,
Of that ingenious artist Mr. Stubbs,
As calling him a horse-painter—how strange,
That Stubbs the title should desire to change!
Yet doth he curses on the occasion utter,
And foolish, quarrel with his bread and butter.
Yes—after Landscape, Gentlemen and Ladies,
This self same Stubbs prodigious mad is,
So quits his Horse, on which the man might ride
To Fame's fair temple, happy and unhurt;
And takes a hobby-horse to gall his pride,
And flings him, like a lubber, in the dirt.
"Peter Pindar"
Lyric Odes, 1782–86

The wide range of arguments for and against eighteenth-century sport provides one explanation of the diversity in approach shown by the artists represented in this exhibition towards their subject. But despite this diversity and despite the fairly frequent appearance of sporting subject matter in more established categories of art such as portraiture or landscape, sporting art was (and is) habitually seen as a distinct and isolated genre. This tendency became more marked as the debate about sport itself became more vocal; sportsmen closed ranks and seemed to form a distinct social group ideologically divorced from the rest of society, and sporting art, in parallel, moved further from the currents of conventionally respectable art. This 'specialization' was reinforced by the introduction of the concept of a specialist painter of sport—one who painted sporting scenes exclusively—in the second or third decade of the eighteenth century. Thereafter "horse-painters" were, in general, viewed with as much derision by connoisseurs of art as were sportsmen by arbiters of social respectability. Ironically, the relatively broad scope for treatment of sporting subjects encouraged by the sporting ideal did little to correct such notions. Sporting painters were apparently expected by their critics to attempt nothing more than a description of sport. John Constable was to pour scorn on "the English Wootton who painted country gentlemen in their wigs and jockey-caps, and top-boots, with packs of hounds, and placed them in Italian landscapes resembling those of Gaspar Poussin,"[1] and George Stubbs's later contribution to landscape and figure painting was mercilessly ridiculed in Dr. Wolcott's ("Peter Pindar") *Lyric Odes*.

The cause of such prejudice cannot of course be explained by the disreputability of sport alone, nor should the effect of such prejudice on the direction of sporting art as a whole be underestimated. Since the increasing specialization of sporting art seems to have been linked to the popular view of its limitations, it is useful to examine both the course of the specialization and the efforts of certain artists later in the century to escape its confines.

Today, sporting pictures are treated very much as a 'special' category of art. In public galleries they tend to be hung in isolated groups, as if they would not mix happily with contemporary portraits or landscapes. They are seen to be of interest primarily to sportsmen (or those curious about sport) and indeed they have always been commissioned or purchased chiefly by sportsmen. Their subject matter, in fact, controls their popularity to a far greater degree than does their quality, explaining, for example, the long neglect of the extraordinarily accomplished work of George Stubbs. Such attitudes are largely a product of habit: the prejudices against sporting art which were born in the eighteenth century remain today, although if distasteful or uninteresting subject matter can indeed cause aesthetic blindness, it should also be conceded that a high proportion of sporting art is unambitiously derivative and sometimes inept. Nevertheless, from its beginnings sporting art has been further isolated in hierarchies of art—if not excluded—by the attitudes of its own patrons.

It was suggested above that sporting pictures could assume a function other than mere decoration; they might be intended to imply a particular personal quality in their owner or to entertain him, his friends, and even his social inferiors.[2] Pictures of other kinds—portraits especially—might have performed similar functions in some circumstances, but the additional notion of art as *equipment* is perhaps peculiar to sporting art. In 1981 the English *Sunday Times* compiled a list of essential sporting accessories that any serious horseman would wish to own; remarkably, perhaps, alongside such items as hunting boots, double bridles, and anti-sweat rugs were listed "sporting pictures."[3] This attitude is by no means exclusively a modern one: from its beginnings sporting art was often acquired by sportsmen who otherwise had no interest in painting. Thomas Thynne, second Viscount Weymouth, who commissioned the several pictures by Wootton in the hall at Longleat, was not concerned with maintaining or adding to any other part of the family collection. According to a Longleat house steward in 1785, he did not add "one good picture to the very few there are at Longleat," had no "Taste for painting," and cared not "a pin about anything but farming and hunting."[4] Moreover the frequent hanging of sporting pictures in the sparse entrance halls of country houses, rather than in the residential rooms, further encouraged the idea that sporting art was in some way on a different plane from the portraits, landscapes, mythologies, or history pictures which hung comfortably in elegant surroundings. An entrance hall was located on the "base or rustic storey . . . dedicated to fox hunters, hospitality, noise, dirt, and business. The next is the floor of taste, expense, state, and parade," wrote Lord Hervey.[5] The consignment of sporting art to a position on the fringes of artistic respectability was perhaps inevitable.

"Horse-painters"—a disparaging term apparently applied indiscriminately to painters of sport—were themselves viewed eventually in a similar light. However, at the beginning of the eighteenth century, when no English artist painted sporting scenes exclusively and when demand for contemporary sporting pictures exceeded supply, [6] the stigma seems to have been less pervasive. Indeed, an expert in animal delineation was highly valued. At various times during the course of his career John Wootton was commissioned to paint horses or other animals in pictures by Eckhardt, Richardson, Jervas, Hudson, Kneller, Dahl, and Gibson.[7] This guaranteed for him a firm niche in artistic society which was denied to later sporting artists. In Gawen Hamilton's group portrait, *A Club of Artists*, 1735 (National Portrait Gallery, London), Wootton stands confidently among such notables of the day as William Kent, George Vertue, John-Michael Rysbrack, and James Gibbs.[8] He was evidently as much at ease with this section of London society as with his artistocratic patrons: for example, to thank the Duke of Richmond for a recent gift of venison, Wootton wrote informally to his benefactor in 1733 and described how he and some friends had gathered

> to partake of your Grace's bounty, and wee did eat and drink your Grace's good health, and each man looked like a new varnished portrait. I had some artists with me but they were observed to draw nothing but corks.[9]

Wootton's rather grand and sociable lifestyle was not repeated by any sporting artist in the latter half of the century; by this time not only were the less savory aspects of sport beginning to discredit artists associated with it, but there was also a glut of people willing to paint sporting scenes. Many lacked professional training and the inevitable decline in standards reflected badly upon the 'horse-painting' profession as a whole. Misguidedly inspired, perhaps, by the prestige acquired by Wootton from his occasional collaborative pictures with major artists, some later sporting painters evidently considered an ability to paint animals the only qualification necessary to enter the profession. Thomas Butler (*fl.* 1750–59) advertised that "He and his assistants, one of which takes views and paints Landskip and figures as well as most, propose to go to several parts of the Kingdom to take Horses and Dogs, Living and Dead Game, Views of Hunts etc."[10] There is evidence here that by the second half of the century sporting artists were having to reassure potential patrons of the quality of the nonsporting elements in their pictures—indeed they were hiring assistants to ensure it.

Ironically, Wootton's prestige had come as much from his own ability as a landscapist as from his expertise in animal painting. This is made quite clear in Vertue's comment that he

> rais'd his reputation & fortune to a great height. being well esteem'd for his skill in *Landskip* painting amongst the professors of Art & in great vogue and favour with many persons of ye greatest Quality. his often visiting of Newmarket in the Seasons produced him much imployment in painting race horses. for which he had good prices. . . ."[11]

Later moves towards specialization by such men as Butler, however, effectively created conditions whereby even the very best sporting artists' ability to paint anything other than horses was barely noticed and often mistrusted. Dr. Wolcott's comments on Stubbs were complemented by those of Lady Carlisle, who wrote of one picture by Stubbs in her collection: "Portrait of a favourite horse; the groom is an admirable likeness; the painter's inability to paint landscape or suffer any other artist to supply his defect, which was requested, renders this work less valuable."[12]

On occasion, Stubbs did allow other artists to supply landscape backgrounds—George Barret (1732–84) in a few instances and Amos Green (1735–1807) in one[13]—but we may assume that he did so reluctantly. Certainly to modern eyes his command of landscape painting is beyond doubt, but his sensitive and precise rendering of English scenery—perhaps most triumphant in the four *Shooting* pictures, exhibited 1767–70 (cat. no. 20), was not liable to please a contemporary taste which preferred either the graver Italianate base of Richard Wilson (1713–82) or the lighter and ultimately less realistic approach of Barret and Francesco Zuccarelli (1702–88). In general, Stubbs was more concerned with relating his main subject matter to its background than with following fashion. A very obvious example of this concern may be found in *Turf, with Jockey up, ca.* 1765 (cat. no. 43), where the closely described anatomies of horse and rider are supported by the uncompromisingly topographical representation of Newmarket Heath and its Rubbing-down House; likewise in the *Zebra, ca.* 1763 (cat. no. 77), the sharp contrast of the animal's black and white stripes is echoed in the alternately dark and light wooded setting. There is here a restrained virtuosity born of considerable self-confidence. Sawrey Gilpin (1733–1807), however, showed an unwarranted lack of confidence in his own ability to provide suitable settings for his paintings of animals. According to the diarist Joseph Farington, he expressed envy of Ben Marshall's (1767–1835) ease in achieving those competent backgrounds "which Stubbs and himself could never venture upon."[14] Certainly Gilpin's collaborations with Barret were frequent and successful (see the engraving after their *Fox Hunting*, 1783, cat. no. 13) but his *Three Hunters in a Rocky Landscape*, 1775 (cat. no. 69), although clearly influenced by Stubbs in subject and setting, is capable throughout and almost certainly by his hand alone.[15]

Ironically, while Gilpin's habitual reliance on collaboration did little to stimulate respect for sporting artists, he, along with Stubbs, actively sought to raise the 'level' of animal painting. Their moves, made primarily for reasons of personal ambition, effectively represent either an effort to escape from the base of the sporting ideal or an attempt to expand it. Stubbs's reported desire "to be considered as an history and portrait painter,"[16] might seem to suggest the former, but both his and Gilpin's insertion of high drama into animal painting had close connections with their own sporting interests and with those of their patrons.

Stubbs's series of pictures portraying confrontations between horses and lions apparently constitutes his most consistent and thorough departure from sporting art. But since Gervase Markham had defined hunting as "a curious search or conquest of one Beast over another, pursued by a natural instinct of enmitie,"[17] it is not difficult to understand either the basis of Stubbs's initial

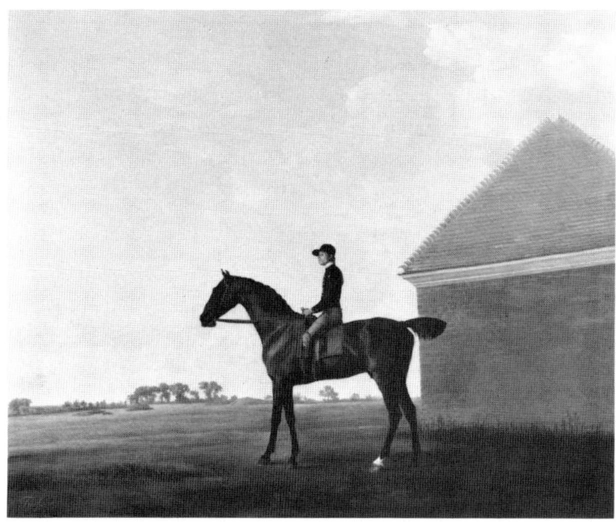

43. George Stubbs: *Turf, with Jockey Up, ca.* 1765

interest in the theme or its attraction to patrons with an enthusiasm for sport (the 2nd Marquess of Rockingham, a noted sportsman, commissioned one of Stubbs's earliest essays in this theme, the vast *Horse Attacked by a Lion, ca.* 1762, which now hangs in the Library Court of the Yale Center for British Art). Violent confrontations between animals had been attempted by earlier sporting artists: Francis Barlow drew both a lion attacked by hounds and a fight between an elephant and a rhinoceros before 1700, and John Wootton's *Fighting Stallions, ca.* 1735, at Longleat was clearly an influence on Stubbs's *Horses Fighting* (see the mezzotint of 1788 after this—cat. no. 80).[18] Nonetheless, Stubbs's dignified yet dramatic treatment of the lion and horse theme was a new departure, for it elevated a subject of potential interest to sportsmen to a level of monumentality that might impress nonsporting patrons, fellow artists, and academies alike. As James Barry put it, such pictures by Stubbs "must rouse and agitate the most inattentive."[19] Unlike the horse portraits or sporting scenes from which Stubbs derived his livelihood, the lion and horse theme provided him with a means of advertising his ability to those outside the sporting world. In so doing, he expanded the range of art which "horse-painters" might reasonably be expected to attempt.

Stubbs's pictorial source for the lion and horse theme —possibly a cast of Giambologna's bronze group, derived from a Graeco-Roman prototype, of a lion attacking a horse[20]—is perhaps of incidental interest, for as contemporary critics were apparently unaware of it and Stubbs himself claimed to look at nature alone for inspi-

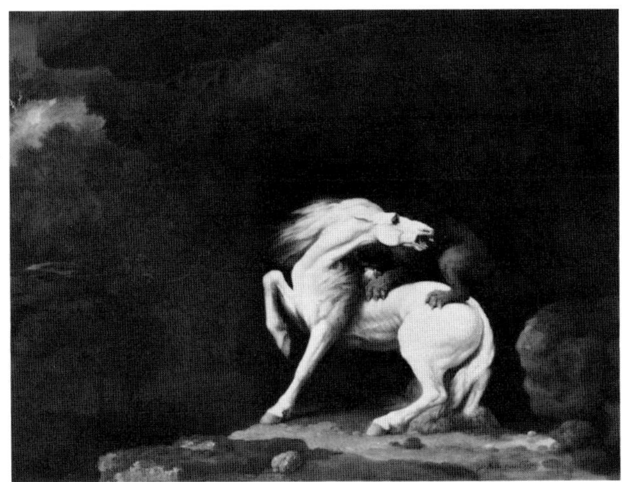

75. George Stubbs: *Horse Attacked by a Lion* (detail), 1770

ration, he was evidently not making a scholarly reference to impress his public further. More relevant is the theme's possible connection both with current written concepts of the sublime and with current theories of the physical manifestation of emotions. In Edmund Burke's *A Philosophical Enquiry into the Origin of our Ideas of the Sublime and Beautiful*, 1757, a specific example of sublimity was given as the transformation of a beautiful creature into a sublime one through the terror of attack,[21] and it has been suggested that one of Stubbs's lion and horse pictures in particular, the *Horse Attacked by a Lion* of 1770 (cat. no. 75), was a precise pictorial articulation of Burke's argument.[22] Whether or not this is the case, Stubbs would have been aware of contemporary notions of the sublime and would have expected his spectators to be so likewise. Horace Walpole's description of the *Horse Frightened by a Lion*, exhibited at the Society of Artists in 1763, as a "sublime essay" suggests that this expectation was fulfilled.[23] Stubbs also seems to have used intellectual reference to elevate his art in his attempt at a close description of the emotional responses of the various horses in the series to their attack or imminent attack. This was not unrelated to ideas of the sublime, for Burke saw "astonishment" to be "the effect of the sublime in its highest degree,"[24] but more directly relevant was Charles Le Brun's seventeenth-century work on the human passions, from which nineteen engravings were in Stubbs's possession.[25] "Expression," wrote Le Brun, "marks the Motions of the Soul and renders visible the Effects of Passion."[26] His attempt to codify an exact visual equivalent for each human emotion—fear, terror, joy, and so forth—aroused much interest in eighteenth-century England. A grasp of Le Brun's ideas and a knowledge of his examples were in fact encouraged as part of the academic training of any aspiring artist.[27] That Stubbs applied lessons learned from Le Brun on the pictorial expression of human emotions to his own description of animal emotions is quite clear: the human head in Le Brun's *Terrour* (cat. no. 85), for example,—gaping eyes, open mouth, flowing hair—provided Stubbs with a model for the terrified horse in his *Horse Attacked by a Lion*, 1770, (cat. no. 75).

If Stubbs's extensive research into the anatomy of animals may be seen as a search for the structure that lies behind form, his interest in Le Brun's concern with the passion that lies behind appearance was wholly consistent. And just as his anatomical work brought him international renown in scientific circles,[28] he must have hoped that his application of theories of human passions to animal paintings would raise his art to the intellectual level of the *istoria*. Certainly, contemporary critics found it hard to avoid a feeling of personal, perhaps protoromantic, involvement with the anguish of Stubbs's terror-stricken horses: "My fibres tremble, and my sinews slack;/I feel his feelings, . . ." wrote Walpole of the Society of Artists exhibit.[29] Subsequent portrayals of animal combat—Stubbs's *Horses Fighting*, 1788 (cat. no. 80), Gilpin's *Horse Frightened by a Snake*, 1792 (cat. no. 70), and James Northcote's *Lion and Snake*, 1799 (cat. no. 72), were all essentially developments of

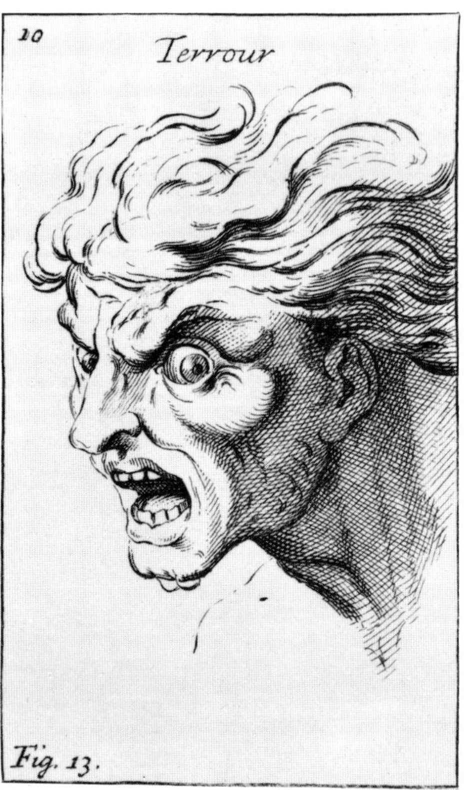

85. Charles Le Brun: *Terrour*

Stubbs's original lion and horse theme, and continued to advance the notion than animal painting might be seen at a human, and thus dignified, level. In parallel with this movement was a written discussion over whether and to what extent animals were capable of emotion and reason. Whereas at the beginning of the century it was generally believed that, in Addison's words, "Animals have nothing like the use of Reason,"[30] John Lawrence could express by the end of the century the prevailing view that the horse "possesses in common with the human race, the reasoning faculty. . . . The body then of the Horse, as well as that of every living creature, is vivified and informed by a soul."[31]

The growing belief that man and animal held certain characteristics in common (of which Stubbs's late work, *A Comparative Anatomical Exposition of the Structure of the Human Body with that of a Tiger and a Common Fowl*, was an extension[32]) had further, diverse ramifications. On the one hand it helps to explain the contemporary concern over cruelty to animals in sport. Once man could believe that animals were capable of fear or reason, the issue of their suffering became less impersonal; as a result, huntsmen were seen to be more barbaric, and so hunting pictures—and, through ill-informed generalization, all sporting pictures—were likewise seen to be less tasteful. Thus whatever 'gains' may have been made in the elevation of animal painting, they were symptomatic of a movement which ultimately and inevitably produced the opposite effect. On the other hand, the newly dignified status of the animal world gave rise to the popularity of pictures in which the mere appearance of an animal—not necessarily engaged in any activity—was thought as worthy a subject of a picture as the human form.

Stubbs's series of frieze-like compositions of mares and foals, painted in the 1760s and 1770s, should be seen primarily in this light. They do not necessarily portray particular animals—and thus are not on the same level as conventional sporting portraits—but seek to demonstrate the simple beauty and even self-assurance of animal form. Obviously, Stubbs's thorough knowledge of the anatomy of the horse would itself have encouraged this kind of detached observation, and his interest in principles of composition—evidenced in this series by his constant experimentation with the play of forms and shapes—would have been another personal motivation for this approach. Furthermore, a sporting connection should be emphasized. In one sense the series is, in Basil Taylor's words, "a monument to [the] . . . English enthusiasm for horse breeding."[33] Indeed, the placing of a vignette of mares and foals under the portrait by

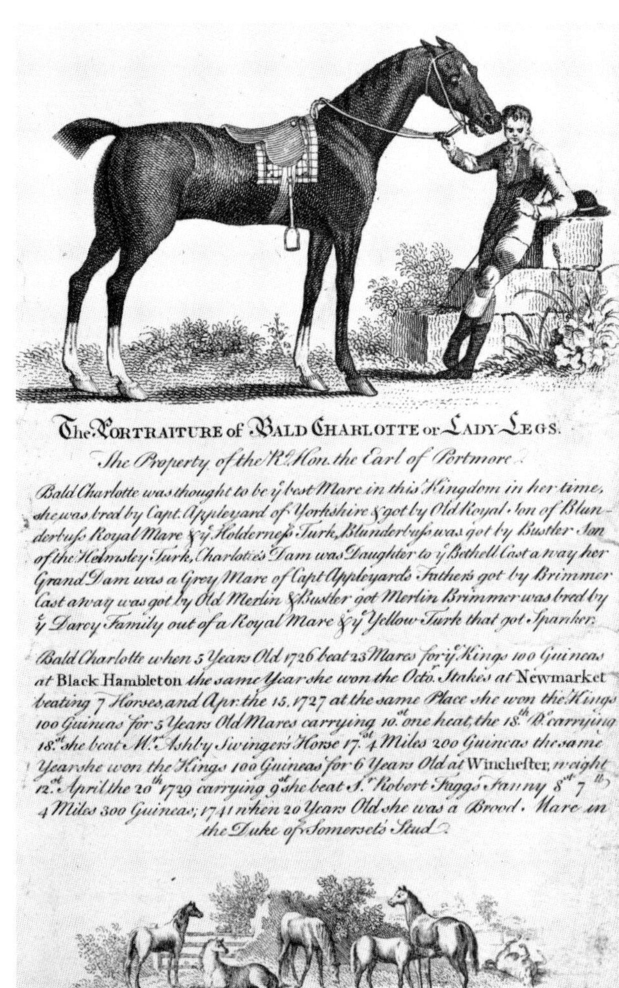

36. Henry Roberts after James Roberts: Plate from *The Sportsman's Pocket Companion*, ca. 1760

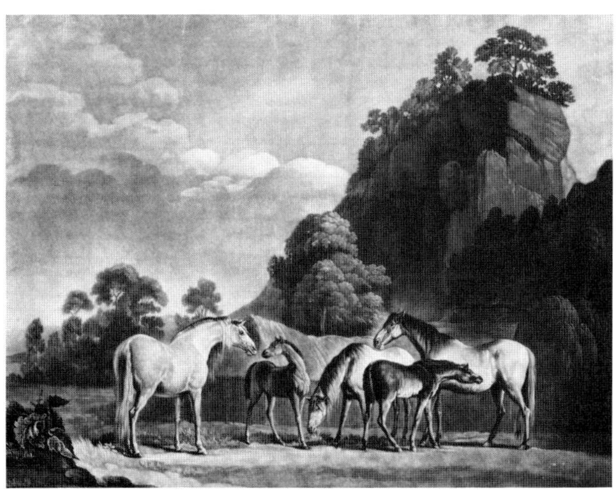

79. Benjamin Green after George Stubbs: *Brood Mares*, 1776

James Roberts of a successful—and thus successfully bred—racehorse, *ca.* 1760 (see *Portraiture of Bald Charlotte or Lady Legs*, engraving by Henry Roberts, cat. no. 36), demonstrates the sporting implication that must also be seen in Stubbs's own undertaking of the theme.[34]

But it was the climate of opinion which ascribed to animals a new, semihuman dignity which helps to explain why Stubbs put as many as seven of these subjects on public exhibition between 1762 and 1776.[35] They were just as much an attempt to raise the level of 'horse-painting' as were his excursions into more overtly exotic subject matter. And while the scenery in which he chose to set these groups was normally reminiscent of restrained and undramatic English countryside[36]—the animals very much at one with nature in the same way that sportsmen were often shown to be—a slightly more exciting setting was selected for the *Brood Mares*, of which Benjamin Green's mezzotint of 1776 is no. 79 in this exhibition. This background was evidently inspired by the same scenery as that depicted in the first of the *Shooting* series (cat. no. 20), known to be Creswell Crags, the limestone cliffs on the edge of the Welbeck estate. The growing taste for craggy backdrops in later eighteenth-century British landscapes, which was related to the development of theories of the Picturesque, undoubtedly encouraged Stubbs's interest in these particular crags. They provided him with the material or at least the inspiration for the backgrounds in countless other pictures.[37] They might be used to heighten the drama of a subject such as the *Horse Attacked by a Lion*, 1770 (cat. no. 75), or, as in the *Brood Mares* and Sawrey Gilpin's adaptation of the theme in *Three Hunters in a Rocky Landscape*, 1775 (cat. no. 69), to add that quality of elevated grandeur which by then could be as reasonably applied to animal subjects as to the history painting, portraiture, and landscape of the time.

Scientific developments stimulated the philosophical changes in attitude towards animals. An upsurge of interest in natural history in the eighteenth century was encouraged partly by improved methods of transportation, which allowed exotic specimens of wildlife to be brought back to England from distant corners of the world and to be put on public display.[38] In the same way that "the menagerie was transformed from its original picturesque or ceremonial circumstance into something like the modern zoological park, which is not just an entertainment, but also a centre of scientific enquiry,"[39] pictures of animals, devoid of narrative, assumed a 'scientific' stature. One such work, Stubbs's *Zebra, ca.* 1763 (cat. no. 77), may appear to have very little to do with what is conventionally categorized as sporting art. But while his contacts with the natural historians of his day (perhaps a predictable consequence of his work as an anatomist) are well known and documented,[40] it should be noted that some of the contemporary interest in exotic animals was sporting, rather than scientific, in origin. Early eighteenth-century natural history manuals tended to be as concerned with recommending suitable methods of hunting unfamiliar animals as with describing their appearance or habits.[41] Although the notion that animals existed either to be used by man or hunted by him regressed in time, sportsmen retained an interest in exotic wildlife that was neither sceintific at heart nor, we might assume, entirely innocent. The list of "Generous Encouragers" of George Edwards's two-volume *Gleanings of Natural History*, 1758–64, for example, included several noted sportsmen;[42] likewise the appearance of a man with a gun in Ibbetson's *Giraffe*, 1796 (cat. no. 84), confirms the links between sport and the new interest in exotica. And, of course, it was a small step from Stubbs's lion and horse series—which, as we have seen, had a firm sporting root—to his single portraits of lions, tigers, leopards, and other beasts of prey.

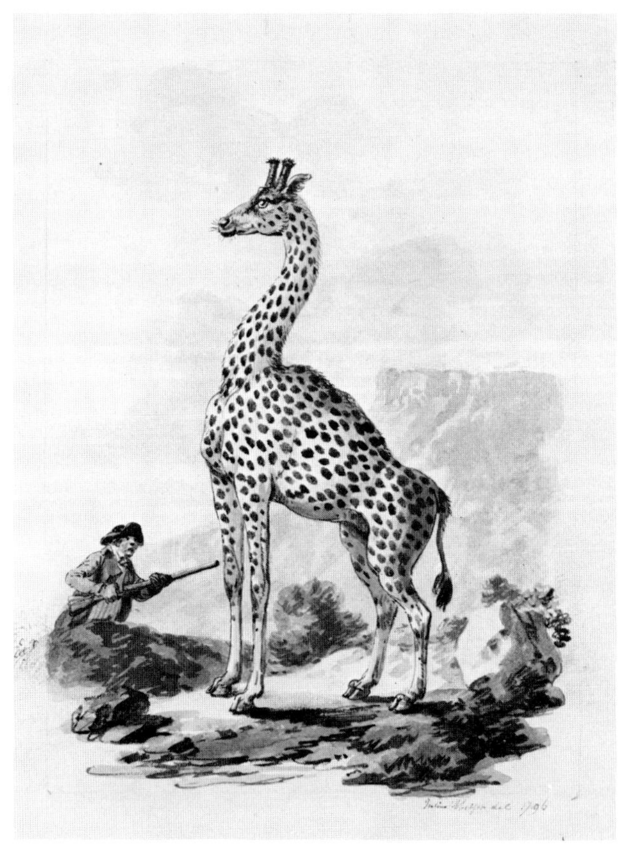

84. Julius Caesar Ibbetson, *Giraffe*, 1796

If Stubbs and Gilpin did indeed wish to correct the prevalent notions of the limitations of 'horse-painting' and its practitioners, they were at least in part successful. Stubbs became an Associate of the Royal Academy in 1780, and his election as a full Academician was denied subsequently only through his own rather stubborn reluctance to comply with the regulation to deposit a diploma picture.[43] Sawrey Gilpin became a full Academician in 1797, when he defeated the portraitist Beechey in the election to fill a vacancy. But Gilpin's success brought disapproval from a writer in the *Oracle* who suggested that "However excellent are the animals of Mr. Gilpin's pencil they would never bring in ten pounds to the Academy—in this view the portrait painter has the preferable claim."[44] Moreover, Stubbs's reversion to horse portraiture in this decade (he accepted a major commission for the *Turf Review* in 1790)[45], which was probably encouraged by a lack of patronage in other areas, further suggests that at the end of the century many of the old prejudices remained. In the early nineteenth century, Henry Alken and John Ferneley were among the most prosperous sporting artists, untroubled by stigma and happy to serve the narrow but lucrative demands of sporting patronage.

The specialization of sporting art tended to diminish its links with other forms of art. James Ward (1769–1859) later continued the tradition of Stubbs and Gilpin in attempting to curb the widening of the gap, but he, like the unaccountably successful Edwin Landseer (1802–73), moved against a hardening trend. The steady growth in the isolation of sporting society, in the sophistication of sporting techniques, and in the accompanying specialist literature were ultimately to exert a stronger influence on sporting taste in art than either the traditional aspects of the sporting ideal or its elevated extensions. Most nineteenth-century sporting art stressed the fun, color, skill, and excitement of a hunt or horse race with little reference to any of those general ideas such as nobility, the experience of nature, or animal emotion which had placed some sporting art close to the mainstream of British art.

The sporting ideal was in a state of particular flux during the eighteenth century in both written and pictorial form. As sport itself expanded, justification was found in old ideals and consolidation in new. The gravity in the work of Wootton, the simplification in Seymour, the placidity in Stubbs, the vigor in Rowlandson, and the diversity in the approach of their many contemporaries were, in part, symptoms of this development. The artists were influenced by a period of considerable transition in sporting history; at the same time they both contributed to the transition and recorded it. The present exhibition attempts to shed some light on the nature of this complex process.

Notes

1. Quoted in E. W. Manwaring, *Italian Landscape in Eighteenth-Century England* (New York, 1925), pp. 72–73.

2. See above, chap. 1.

3. *The Sunday Times Colour Magazine*, May 10, 1981, pp. 52–53.

4. Quoted in letter from Hon. Hester Hoare to Harriett Anne Bishop, April 11, 1785, in *The Parham Park Papers*, unpublished, vol. 2, p. 13.

5. Lord Hervey, quoted in Williams, *Life in Georgian England*, p. 31.

6. See Walker, *Sporting Art*, p. 60.

7. See George E. Kendall, "Notes on the Life of John Wootton," *Walpole Society* XXI (1932–33), pp. 23–42.

8. Others portrayed are Hans Hysing, Michael Dahl, Joseph Goupy, Charles Bridgeman, Matthew Robinson, Bernard Baron, and William Thomas.

9. Quoted in W. T. Whitley, *Artists and their Friends in England 1700–99* (London, 1928), vol. 1, p. 78.

10. Ibid., pp. 78–79.

11. Vertue III (*Walpole Society* XXII), p. 34.

12. Lady Carlisle's MS catalogue of paintings at Castle Howard, quoted in Parker, *Mr. Stubbs the Horse Painter*, p. 158.

13. See Egerton, *British Sporting and Animal Paintings*, pp. 82–83, and Francis Russell, "Lord Torrington and Stubbs: A Footnote," *Burlington Magazine* CXXII (1980), pp. 250–53.

14. *Diary of Joseph Farington*, ed. J. Greig, vol. 2, (London, 1923), pp. 216–17.

15. See Egerton, *British Sporting and Animal Paintings*, p. 118.

16. Letter from Josiah Wedgwood to Thomas Bentley, September 14, 1780.

17. Markham, *Country Contentments*, p. 3.

18. Barlow's *Lion Attacked by Hounds*, sold Christie's, 2 March 1976, no. 7; *Elephant and Rhinoceros*, Witt Collection, no. 2376. For Wootton's *Fighting Stallions* at Longleat, see *Country Life*, April 22, 1949, p. 928, and December 4, 1958, p. 1291.

19. *The Works of James Barry* (London, 1809), vol. 1, p. 23.

20. Basil Taylor originally suggested that Stubbs's inspiration was the antique marble sculpture in the Palazzo dei Conservatori in Rome of a lion attacking a horse, which he could have seen on his visit to Italy in 1754 (see "George Stubbs: The 'Lion and Horse Theme' ", *Burlington Maga-*

zine CVII (1965), pp. 81–6). More recently it has been argued that this inspiration came from an indirect source: either from the engraving by Adamo Ghisi of a lion attacking a horse, or from a cast of the bronze group by Giambologna of a similar subject—both evidently based on the very different appearance of the Roman sculpture before its radical restoration in 1594. In showing the horse's head turned back towards its attacker in all 17 of his known works on this theme, Stubbs follows Ghisi and Giambologna rather than the restored sculpture which has the horse's head facing away from the lion (see *The Tate Gallery 1976–8. Illustrated Catalogue and Acquisitions*, 1979, p. 16).

It should be noted in addition that there is a drawing attributed to Stubbs in the collection of the Huntington Library and Art Gallery depicting a lion attacking a bull: this is evidently a detailed sketch taken from the *Lion Attacking a Bull* made by Giambologna as a pendant for his lion and horse group and also derived from a Graeco-Roman prototype. [Giambologna's groups are both reproduced in Charles Avery and Anthony Redcliffe, *Giambologna 1529–1608* (Arts Council exhibition catalogue, 1978), p. 187.] If the attribution of the drawing to Stubbs is correct, it may be suggested that he saw Giambologna's *Lion Attacking a Horse* when he saw its pendant, the subject of his sketch.

21. Edmund Burke, *A Philosophical Enquiry into the Origin of our Ideas of the Sublime and Beautiful*, ed. James T. Boulton (London, 1958), p. 66.

22. See Robert R. Wark, "A Horse and Lion Painting by George Stubbs," *Bulletin of the Associates in Fine Arts at Yale University* XXII, no. 1 (1955), pp. 1–7.

23. From a poem for the *Public Advertiser*, 1763, in Walpole, *Anecdotes of Painting*, vol. 4, p. 111.

24. Burke, *The Origin of the Sublime*, p. 57.

25. See catalogue of sale of Stubbs's collection, Peter Coxe, May 26–27, 1807, First Day's sale no. 9, "Le Brun's Passions in 19 engravings, half bound." Note also no. 1: "Twelve coloured Prints of the Passions" in the same section entitled "Engravings by Mr. Stubbs, Bartolozzi, &c."

26. Charles Le Brun, *Characters of the Passions*, English ed. (London, 1701), p. 2.

27. See Robert Sayer, *The Compleat Drawing-Book* (London, 1757).

28. See *George Stubbs, Anatomist and Animal Painter*, Tate Gallery, 1976, passim.

29. Walpole, *Anecdotes of Painting*, vol. 4, p. 111.

30. *The Spectator*, no. 121, July 1711.

31. Lawrence, *A Treatise on Horses*, vol. 2, p. 78.

32. Stubbs was occupied with this work from 1795 until his death. The drawings are now in the Mellon Collection.

33. Basil Taylor, *Stubbs*, 2d ed. (London, 1975), p. 26.

34. The Roberts engraving is unlikely to have been made later than 1760. It comes from *The Sportsman's Pocket Companion* (undated), largely a guide to famous racehorses from 1709 to 1753. There are no examples extant of Stubbs's mares and foals theme dated before 1761, but since Stubbs is more likely to have influenced Roberts than vice versa, Stubbs may have made his first attempts at the theme in the 1750s.

35. Society of Artists 1762: no. 110; 1764: no. 114; 1765: no. 127; 1766: no. 163; 1768: no. 165, no. 112; Royal Academy 1776: no. 294.

36. Ten examples are conveniently reproduced in Parker, *Mr. Stubbs the Horse Painter*, p. 57.

37. Stubbs's use of Creswell Crags as a source for his landscape backgrounds is the subject of a forthcoming article in the *Burlington Magazine* by Judy Egerton.

38. See Taylor, *Stubbs*, pp. 30–31.

39. Basil Taylor, *Animal Painting in England from Barlow to Landseer* (Harmondsworth, 1955), p. 33.

40. See *George Stubbs, Anatomist and Animal Painter*, passim.

41. See (Thomas Boreman) *Three Hundred Animals* (London, 1730).

42. For example, Peter Delmé, Henry Hoare, and the Duke of Richmond: patrons of Seymour, Wootton, and Stubbs, respectively.

43. Taylor, *Stubbs*, p. 19.

44. Quoted in *British Sporting Painting*, The Arts Council, p. 19.

45. The commission was for a series of portraits depicting famous racehorses, to be exhibited and engraved by his son George Townley Stubbs. The project was not completed.

The Exhibition and Checklists:

The exhibition is divided into five sections, each of which identifies a distinct method of approach to the portrayal of sport in eighteenth-century British art. They represent diverse expressions of the sporting ideal, whose nature has been examined in the preceding essay.

A brief discussion of each section follows and is accompanied by a checklist. Each object is described in the checklist by artist, title, date (if known), and dimensions in inches (with metric equivalents in brackets), height before width. Medium is oil on canvas unless otherwise stated. If mentioned in the main text of this catalogue, a page reference is also supplied. An asterisk beside a catalogue number denotes that the object is illustrated. A full catalogue entry for most objects may be found in the series: *Sport in Art and Books: The Paul Mellon Collection*, published by the Tate Gallery for the Yale Center for British Art, 1978–81.

The following abbreviations are used:

Egerton—Judy Egerton, *British Sporting and Animal Paintings 1655–1867*

Egerton & Snelgrove—Judy Egerton and Dudley Snelgrove, *British Sporting and Animal Drawings 1500–1850*

Snelgrove—Dudley Snelgrove, *British Sporting and Animal Prints 1658–1874*

Podeschi—John B. Podeschi, *Books on the Horse and Horsemanship 1400–1941*

With the exception of cat. no. 75, all objects belong either to the collection of Mr. Paul Mellon or to the Yale Center for British Art. Those from the Yale Center have a "B" accession number. Paintings and drawings lent by Mr. Mellon have a "PM" number; prints on loan are marked "PM" but are not numbered.

Index of Artists

Section I. *Sport in Portraiture*

The paintings in the first section of the exhibition are perhaps removed from conventional notions of what constitutes sporting art. They are not *about* sport, but make a reference to sport with a particular purpose: the spectator is asked to associate the sitter with the ideal benefits of sport, which, as we have seen, had been developed in literary form and had become embedded in the eighteenth-century consciousness. When a sporting accessory—a gun, a hunting costume, a horse—was introduced into a portrait or when sport was made the theme of a conversation-piece, an eighteenth-century spectator would be expected to recall one or more of the advantages that sport was said to offer and apply them mentally to the subject.

The guns and dogs that are shown beside Windham Quin (cat. no. 10), Thomas Graham (cat. no. 1, cover ill.) and Edward Haytley's unidentified man (cat. no. 5) are intended to perform this function. Quin and Graham were known as keen sportsmen of their day, but Slaughter and Allan refer to their hobby without describing it. William Hogarth, likewise, might use an object—perhaps a book or a globe—to refer to the hobby or interest of a sitter in order to convey a sense of his character more thoroughly than by merely recording his appearance. William Dobson's *Endymion Porter, ca.* 1643–45 (The Tate Gallery, London), is an early example of sporting reference in English portraiture, painted in the first half of the seventeenth century when the articulation of a sporting ideal in literature was beginning in earnest. The simple format of Dobson's picture, and those of Slaughter, Allan, and Haytley, remained popular throughout the late seventeenth, eighteenth, and early nineteenth centuries. In later years this approach lost favor, however, partly through the increasing awareness of the less wholesome aspects of sport. During the eighteenth century, written discussion of the potential side effects of sport—financial ruin, impolite behavior, or cruelty to animals—would eventually make a general reference to sport in a portrait undesirably ambiguous.

Bifrons Park (cat. no. 2), painted early in the century when no such ambiguity was likely, is also concerned with the general implications of the sporting ideal. It is a country house portrait into which a sporting party is introduced to emphasize the widely beneficial features of country life. Whether the members of the party are intended to be portraits of particular people or *staffage*, their engagement in sport, and all that this implied, provides a suitable element of narrative.

Other pictures might refer to particular aspects of the sporting ideal. Thus in George Morland's *Party Angling* (cat. no. 6) and *The Anglers' Repast* (cat. no. 7) the emphasis is on the sitters' lighthearted enjoyment both of each others' company and of nature. An eighteenth-century spectator's knowledge that these were ideal attributes of sport would encourage his involvement in the scenes: here, as in the conversation pieces of Hayman or Mortimer (cat. nos. 4, 8), sport is not intended to be the main subject, but because of its associations provides a suitable thematic element aimed at enhancing our understanding of the characters portrayed.

Checklist

1.* David Allan: *Thomas Graham (afterwards 1st Baron Lynedoch) in Rome*, 1769. 54 1/2 x 38 3/4 (138.5 x 98.5 cm.). B1981.25.14. Egerton 128

2.* British School: *Bifrons Park, Kent, ca.* 1705–10. 61 1/2 x 91 1/2 (86.8 x 132.5 cm.). B1977.14.83. See *Country Houses in Great Britain*, Yale Center for British Art, 1979, no. 10 See p. 13

3. Arthur Devis: *Leak Okeover, Rev. John Allen, and Capt. Chester in the Grounds of Okeover Hall, Staffordshire*, 1745–47. 38 1/2 x 48 1/2 (97.7 x 123.2 cm.). B1981.25.746. Egerton 58

4. Francis Hayman: *George Rogers with his Wife and ?Sister, ca.* 1750–55. 41 x 39 (104 x 99 cm.). B1981.25.327. Egerton 55

5. Edward Haytley: *An Unknown Sportsman*, 1752. 20 x 14 (51 x 35.5 cm.). B1976.7.37. Egerton 64

6. George Morland: *A Party Angling*, before 1789. 25 x 30 (63.5 x 76.2 cm.). PM No. 840. Egerton 167

7.* George Morland: *The Anglers' Repast*, before 1789. 25 x 30 (63.5 x 76.2 cm.). PM No. 841. Egerton 167

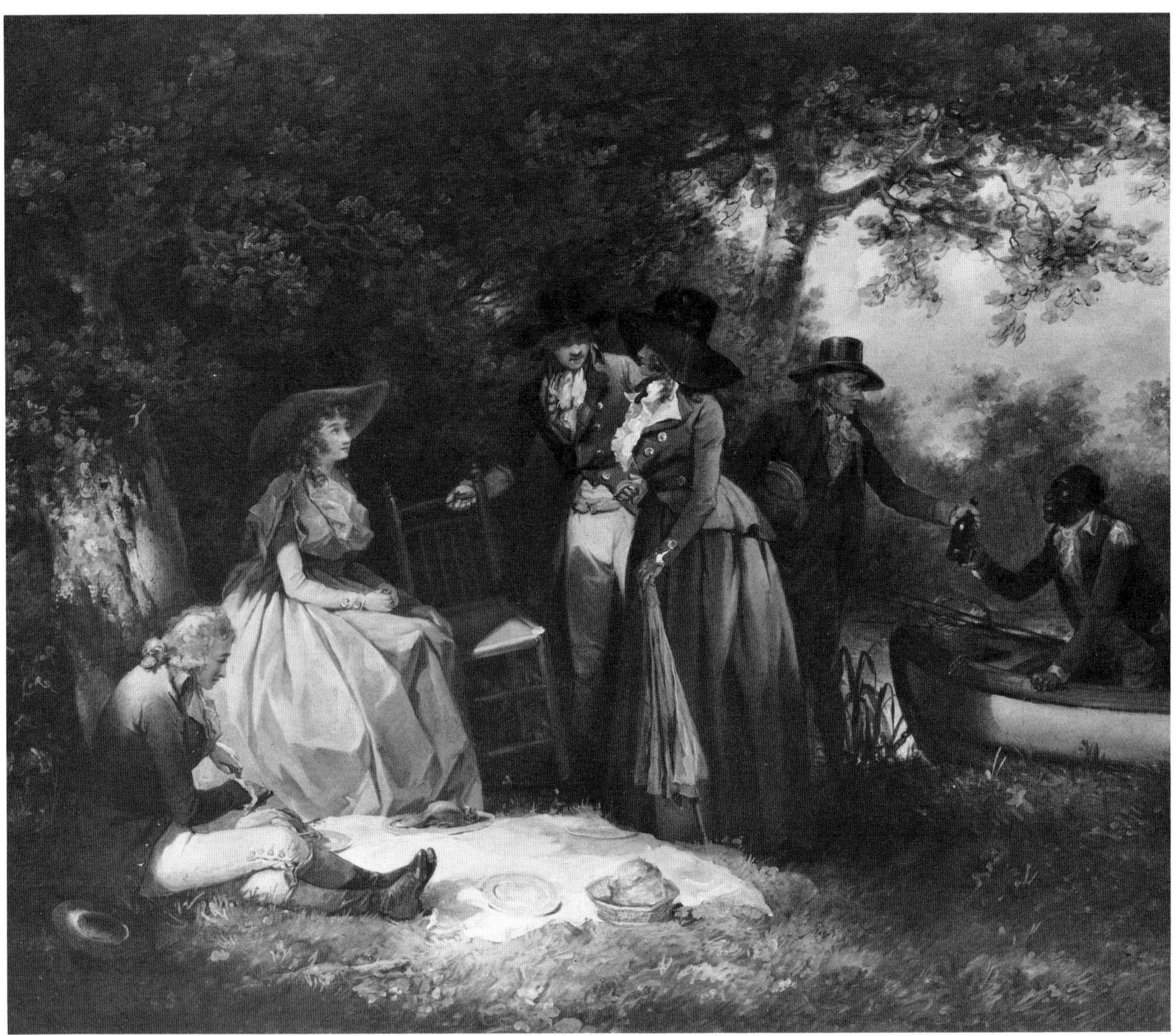

7. George Morland:
The Anglers' Repast, before 1789

8. John Hamilton Mortimer: *The Artist and his Brother Charles, after Woodcock-shooting, with their Father Thomas Mortimer*, early 1760s. 30 x 25 (76.2 x 63.5 cm.). B1981.25.466. Egerton 125

9. Francis Sartorius: *John Corbet, Robert Leighton and John Kynaston, Members of the Shrewsbury Hunt*, 1779. 37 3/4 x 57 1/2 (96 x 146 cm.). B1981.25.552. Egerton 121

10. Stephen Slaughter: *Windham Quin with Gun, Dog, and Game, ca.* 1745. 40 1/8 x 50 5/8 (102 x 128.5 cm.). B1981.25.574. Egerton 40 See p. 10

11. George Stubbs: *The Countess of Coningsby in the Costume of the Charlton Hunt, ca.* 1760. 25 x 29 1/4 (63.5 x 74.5 cm.). B1981.25.620. Egerton 66

Section 2. *Traditional Ideals*

The origin of many elements of the sporting ideal predated the establishment in the early eighteenth century of a flourishing British school of art devoted to the representation of sporting scenes. The paintings, prints, and drawings in this section of the exhibition are those in which sport is unequivocally the main subject but in which it is presented in an overtly idealized manner. They were influenced by and perpetuated the traditional ideals of sport whose contemporary discussion in literary form had roots in earlier centuries. Seventeenth-century argument over the preferability of a court or a country life was superseded in the eighteenth century by more advanced urban and rural ideologies. Sport—despite its courtly origins—lay at the heart of the latter.

Stubbs's four shooting scenes (cat. no. 20), for example, embody the ideals of health, relaxation, and the experience of nature. They exude a peaceful air; there is no hint of urgency in the actions of the sportsmen, even when, in the third scene, they are shooting game. They are at one with the lush countryside that surrounds them; even the depiction in the first scene of part of Creswell Crags is given no hint of the drama it was to assume when used in some of the artist's later lion and horse scenes. James Ross's much earlier *A Meet of Foxhounds* (cat. no. 15) was intended to evoke a similar response: Ross shows an unhurried hunting party pausing for a moment's healthy enjoyment of a rich landscape, which has only a loose topographical base.

Such idealization of activity or setting is taken to a greater extreme in other pictures, with a further function. In *The Death of the Hare* (cat. no. 12) the Italianate background and formal poses of the sportsmen provide an air of grandeur and dignity which serves to suggest the 'nobility' of sport and its participants. There is a

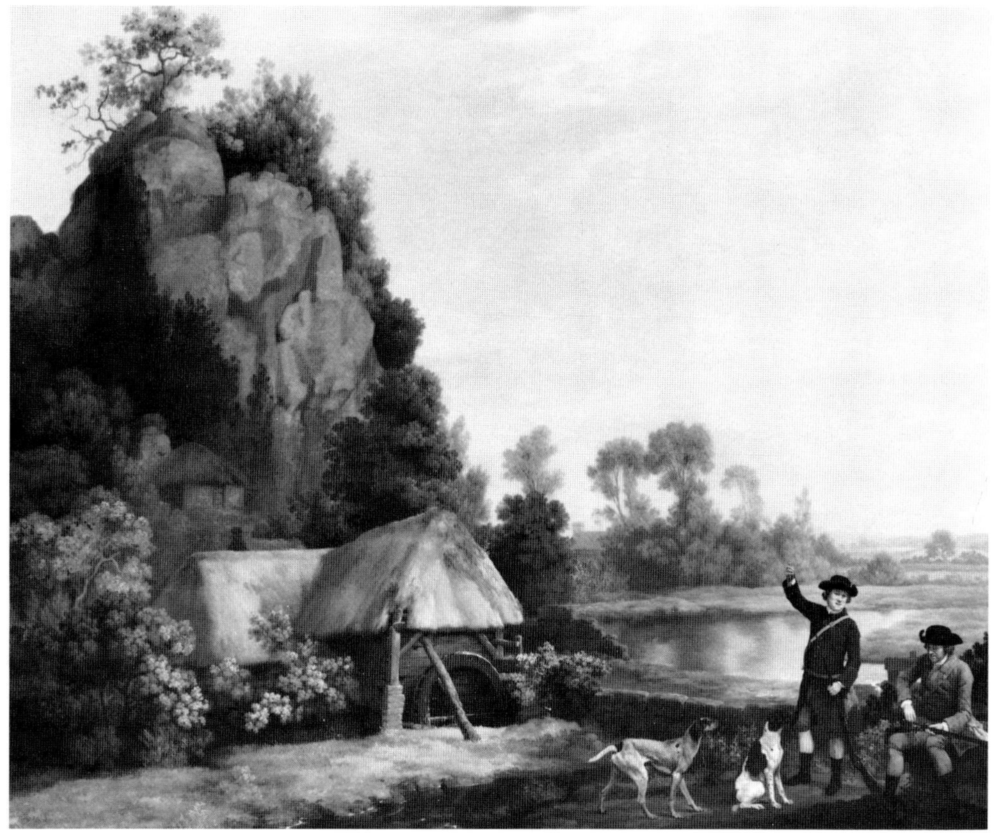

20(i). George Stubbs: *Two Gentlemen going a shooting, with a view of Creswell Crags: taken on the spot,* exh. 1767

similar implication in Wootton's depiction of Sir Robert Walpole's hunting party (engraving by Lerpinière: cat. no. 27, back cover ill.).

Too rigid a matching of subject matter to particular ideals should be avoided, especially when an apparent allusion to an ideal was made indirectly. Thus Seymour's *Three Riders Following Hounds Towards a Five-Barred Gate* (cat. no. 18), although idealized pictorially, may be read as a simple descriptive representation of a sporting episode. A further interpretation, that the jumping of the gate will demand skill in horsemanship—a traditional element of the sporting ideal—may be made only with caution. Likewise the military connotation of sport, an ideal given clear pictorial expression in Jan Wyck's *Hare Hunting* (cat. no. 28), is stated only discreetly in Wootton's grandiose *George I at Newmarket* (cat. no. 25; see pp. 16,17). Evidently, eighteenth-century spectators were themselves occasionally uncertain to what degree traditional ideals were present in some pictures. Stubbs's grave portrait of the racehorse *Shark* (cat. no. 22, ill. p. 4) presents horse and trainer as noble objects in an imaginary and quiet lakeside setting. While one writer, John Lawrence, found "that sober attitude and character" of Stubbs's representation wholly realistic, he conceded that "I have been told particularly, that his Shark is quite a different thing to the real Horse . . . a fine, gallant, gay, and airy Stallion."

Checklist

12.* British School: *The Death of the Hare, ca.* 1765–70. 60 x 99 (152.5 x 251.5 cm.). B1981.25.267. Egerton 101 See p. 15

13. After Sawrey Gilpin and George Barret: *Fox Hunting*, 1783. Colored engraving. Figures by F. Bartolozzi; landscape by T. Morris. 14 5/8 x 20 1/4 (372 x 514 mm.). PM. Snelgrove: Gilpin no. 5 See p. 31

14.* John Henry Muntz: *Landscape with Sportsmen and Dogs Resting*, 1779. Pen & ink & watercolor. 8 5/8 x 11 3/16 (219 x 285 mm.). B1975.4.1351. Egerton & Snelgrove: Muntz no. 1 See p. 12

15. James Ross: *A Meet of Foxhounds*, 1732. 40 1/4 x 49 7/8 (102.2 x 126.7 cm.). PM No. 1774. Egerton 53

16.* Thomas Rowlandson: *A Stag Hunt in the West Country*. Pen & ink & watercolor. 5 1/4 x 9 (134 x 229 mm.). B1981.25.2675. Egerton & Snelgrove: Rowlandson no. 9 See p. 12

17. James Seymour: *The Stables and Two Famous Running Horses Belonging to the Duke of Bolton*, 1747. 24 1/2 x 29 1/4 (62 x 74.5 cm.). PM No. 798. Egerton 50 See p. 14

18. James Seymour: *Three Riders Following Hounds Towards a Five-Barred Gate, ca.* 1735–40. 28 x 90 (71 x 228 cm.). PM No. 3084. Egerton 46

19.* James Seymour: *Mr. Peter Delmé's Hounds on the Hampshire Downs*, 1738. 40 x 50 (101.5 x 127 cm.). PM No. 5018. Egerton 45 See p. 11

20.* George Stubbs: *Shooting*: a series of 4, exhibited 1767–70. Each 39 x 49 (99 x 124.5 cm.). B1976.7.85–88. Egerton 79 See pp. 10–11, 21 (note 6), 34

21. After George Stubbs: *Shooting*: a series of 4, 1769–71. Engravings by William Woollett. Each 17 7/16 x 21 7/8 (444 x 557 mm.). PM. Snelgrove: Stubbs no. 5

22.* George Stubbs: *Shark with his Trainer Price*, 1775. 40 x 50 (101.5 x 127 cm.). PM No. 2023. Egerton 85

23. Thomas Weaver: *Coursing*, 1800. Pen & ink & watercolor. 9 3/8 x 12 1/4 (238 x 311 mm.). PM No. LGD 73/12/14/414. Egerton & Snelgrove: Weaver no. 1 See p. 14

24. John Wootton: *A Fox Hunt, ca.* 1730–40. 45 x 69 (114.25 x 175.25 cm.). B1981.25.696. Egerton 21

25.* John Wootton: *George I at Newmarket, ca.* 1717. 50 1/8 x 67 1/16 (127.3 x 170.3 cm.). B1981.25.698. Egerton 15 See pp. 16, 17

26.* John Wootton: *Preparing for the Hunt, ca.* 1740–50. 47 x 49 (119.5 x 124.5 cm.). B1981.25.704. Egerton 30 See p. 15

27.* After John Wootton: *A Hunting Piece*, 1778. Engraving by D. Lerpinière. 17 x 23 (432 x 583 mm.). PM. Snelgrove: Wootton no. 3

28.* Jan Wyck: *Hare Hunting, ca.* 1690. 56 x 48 (142.2 x 122 cm.). B1981.25.725. Egerton 6 See pp. 10, 16

Section 3. *New Ideals*

Many eighteenth-century British sporting pictures would not have been of great interest to anyone other than the sportsman. They articulated the more modern elements of the sporting ideal, describing particular aspects of sport which members of sporting society celebrated regardless of any debate that might surround their activity. Perfection in breeding and technique, sporting success, and the opportunity for socializing and general enjoyment were the consistent themes in the art and literature of the period which made up this 'internal' ideology. In pictorial form its expression was ostensibly topographical, but could range from the dignity and precision of George Stubbs's portrait of the racehorse *Turf* (cat. no. 43) or Richard Roper's dry historical record of the outcome of a particular horsematch (cat. no. 37), to the lighthearted presentation of a typical rather than an actual sporting scene, as in Frederick George Byron's *Shooting Party* pair (cat. nos. 29, 30).

Portraiture of successful racehorses provided lucrative business for artists and a permanent record of a breeding and sporting achievement for owners. A horse's pedigree was highly regarded, and the accompanying and constant interest in a horse's stud potential explains, for example, the combination of William Shaw's close examination of the appearance of the stallion *Blank* (cat. no. 41) with a narrative of the animal's approach towards a mare. Stubbs's horse portraits tend to be less anecdotal and probably more accurate in description. While occasionally introducing overtly idealized elements into horse portraiture (see *Shark*, cat. no. 22 in section 2) his thorough knowledge of horse anatomy brought him several commissions for more strictly topographical sporting pictures. His portrait of *Eclipse* (cat. no. 44), the most successful racehorse of the eighteenth century, both supplies a precise record of the animal's appearance and perpetuates the sportsman's ideal of perfection in breeding.

The sheer enjoyment provided by sport was stressed as one of its main attractions in the latter half of the century. The anthologies of boisterous hunting songs and irreverent poetry which appeared in profusion helped to formulate an ideal of jollity which is also conveyed in many sporting pictures. James Dunthorne's unlikely (but supposedly historically accurate) sporting scene (cat. no. 31) expresses the fun of sport with a slight sense of absurdity that is encouraged by the undeliberately awry pictorial perspective. With greater artistic accomplishment Thomas Rowlandson portrays a lively hunt breakfast (cat. no. 39), full of the implication of the vigorous enjoyment to follow. The affable conversations depicted in three of Wootton's pictures (cat. nos. 46, 48, 49) suggest the ideal of social mixing, as does the Newmarket scene by Peter Tillemans (cat. no. 45), in which other aspects of the lively bustle of a sporting event are also suggested.

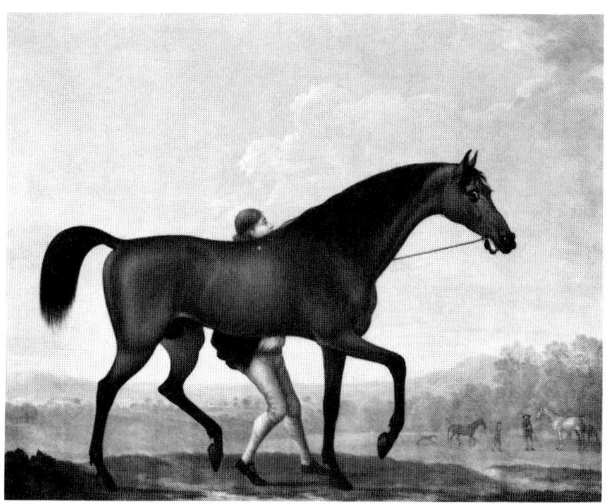

41. William Shaw: *The Duke of Ancaster's Bay Stallion Blank Walking Towards a Mare, ca.* 1770

Checklist

29.* Frederick George Byron, *Shooting Party Setting Out*, 1789. Pen & ink & watercolor. 16 3/4 x 21 (426 x 535 mm.). PM No. 66/11/2/15. Egerton & Snelgrove: Byron no. 1
See p. 19

30.* Frederick George Byron, *Shooting Party Returning Home*, 1789. Pen & ink & watercolor. 16 5/8 x 21 5/16 (422 x 541 mm.). PM No. 66/11/2/16 Egerton & Snelgrove: Byron no. 1
See p. 19

31. James Dunthorne: *John Sidey and his Hounds at a Farmhouse near Hadleigh, Suffolk*, 1765. 35 1/2 x 54 (90 x 137 cm.). PM No. 18. Egerton 107

32. George Garrard: *The Duke of Hamilton's Disguise, with Jockey up*, 1786. 33 1/2 x 42 1/2 (85 x 108 cm.). PM No. 724. Egerton 158

33. After George Morland: *Fox Hunting: Going Out*, 1800. Mezzotint by Edward Bell printed in color and colored by hand. 20 x 25 3/4 (508 x 653 mm.). PM. Snelgrove: Morland no. 1 See p. 18

34. After George Morland: *Fox Hunting: Going into Cover*, 1801. Mezzotint by Edward Bell printed in color and colored by hand. 20 x 25 3/4 (508 x 653 mm.). PM. Snelgrove: Morland no. 1 See p. 18

35. After George Morland: *Fox Hunting: The Death*, 1800. Mezzotint by Edward Bell printed in color and colored by hand. 20 x 25 3/4 (508 x 653 mm.). PM. Snelgrove: Morland no. 1 See p. 27

36.* After James Roberts: *Portraiture of Bald Charlotte or Lady Legs*, *ca.* 1760. Engraving by Henry Roberts. 8 1/4 x 5 1/4 (209 x 133 mm.). PM. Snelgrove: Roberts no. 10 See p. 34

37. Richard Roper: *The Match between Aaron and Driver at Maidenhead, August 1754*, [1] *Driver Winning the First Heat*, *ca.* 1754. 35 x 48 (89 x 122 cm.). PM No. 6301. Egerton 105 (1) See p. 19

38. Thomas Ross: *Netting Partridges*. Pen & gray wash. 7 5/8 x 11 3/4 (193 x 289 mm.). PM No. LGD 73/12/14/267. Egerton & Snelgrove: Ross no. 1 See p. 18

39. Thomas Rowlandson: *Breakfast before the Hunt ca.* 1785–90. Pen & ink & brown and blue wash. 5 x 8 (127 x 202 mm.). PM No. 64/1/9/3. Egerton & Snelgrove: Rowlandson no. 2

40. After James Seymour: *Death of the Fox*, 1794. Mezzotint by Thomas Burford. 9 7/8 x 13 3/4 (250 x 248 mm.). B1970.3.842. Snelgrove: Seymour no. 4

41.* William Shaw: *The Duke of Ancaster's Bay Stallion Blank Walking Towards a Mare*, *ca.* 1770. 40 1/8 x 50 1/8 (101.9 x 127.3 cm.). PM No. 8507. Egerton 109

42. Thomas Spencer: *Scipio, Colonel Roche's Spotted Hunter*, *ca.* 1750. 39 x 52 3/4 (99 x 134 cm.). PM No. 4576. Egerton 56

43.* George Stubbs: *Turf, with Jockey up*, *ca.* 1765. 39 x 49 (99.1 x 124.5 cm.). B1981.25.621. Egerton 76A See p. 31

44.* George Stubbs: *Eclipse*, *ca.* 1770. 25 1/2 x 30 3/4 (64.7 x 78 cm.). PM No. 6292. Egerton 82 See p. 18

45. Peter Tillemans: *View of the Round Course at Newmarket, with Racehorses Going to Start for the King's Plate*, *ca.* 1720. 34 1/2 x 39 1/4 (87 x 99.75 cm.). B1981.25.629. Egerton 33 See p. 17

46. John Wootton: *The Duke of Rutland's Bonny Black*, *ca.* 1715. 30 x 48 1/2 (76.2 x 123.2 cm.). B1981.25.695. Egerton 12 See p. 19

47. John Wootton: *A Grey Spotted Hound*, *ca.* 1738. 40 x 50 (101.5 x 127 cm.). B1981.25.701. Egerton 28

48. John Wootton: *Lord Portmore Watching Racehorses at Exercise on Newmarket Heath*, *ca.* 1735. 26 5/8 x 49 (67.6 x 124.4 cm.). B1981.25.706. Egerton 25 See p. 22 (note 23)

49. John Wootton: *A Nobleman Arriving to Inspect Racehorses at Newmarket*, *ca.* 1735. 26 1/2 x 46 1/8 (67.3 x 117.1 cm.). PM No. 6555. Egerton 26

Section 4. *Humor*

The pleasure given by rural sport to its participants often received pictorial and written expression with a specifically humorous emphasis. The jollity that became an important ingredient of the sporting ideal in the latter half of the eighteenth century focused on particular themes which were both developed in literary form and articulated in the prints and drawings which appear in this section of the exhibition. They range from the jingoistic satire of urban life to the distinctly irreverent celebration of the private humor of sporting society, which was often tinged with a hint of healthy self-mockery.

Thomas Rowlandson is well represented here. The keenness both of his wit and draughtsmanship brought a wide demand for his depictions of fictional sporting scenes or incidents which perpetuated the various themes of sporting humor. His *Enraged Vicar* (cat. no. 61), *Hunt Subscription* (cat. no. 62), and *Dinner* (cat. no. 63) are intended purely to amuse and entertain his spectators. The *Bookmaker and Client Outside the Ram Inn, Newmarket* (cat. no. 60), however, possibly carries a moralistic overtone (see p. 26).

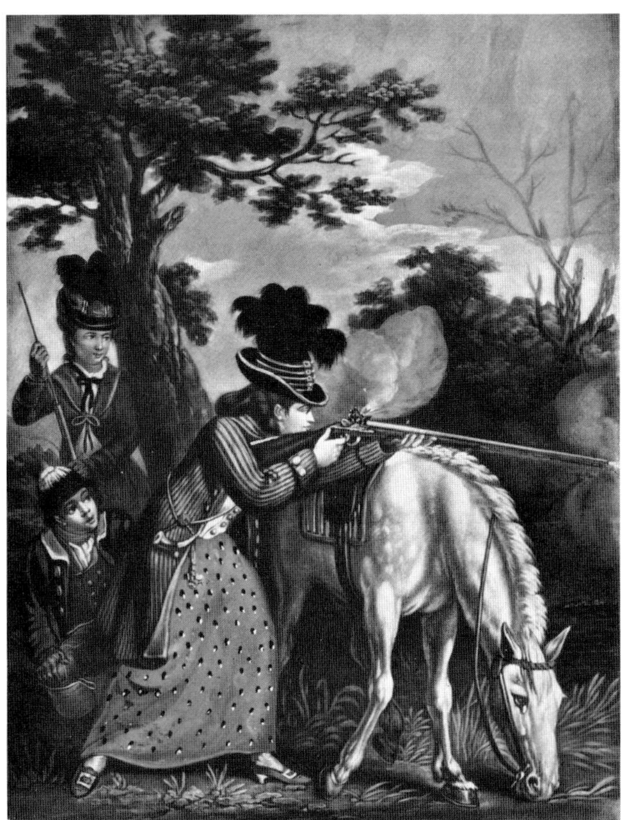

53. John Collet: *The Ladies' Shooting Poney*, 1780

The popular connection between sporting and courting was frequently used as a medium for pictorial humor in the eighteenth century. *The Amorous Sportsman* after Francis Wheatley (cat. no. 66) and Marcellus Laroon's *Man and Woman with a Bag of Game* (cat. no. 58), are examples of works which use sporting mythology to provide a means of humorous narrative. Likewise, in the oil painting *The Joys of the Chase* (cat. no. 52) John Collet uses a sporting scenario to extend his favorite theme of the triumph of heartless women over clumsy men. The same artist's *The Ladies' Shooting Poney* (cat. no. 53) and H. F. B. Gravelot's *The Sporting Lady* (cat. no. 57) reflect contemporary sportsmen's amusement at the occasional involvement of women in traditionally 'manly' sports.

Many of these works might have delighted sportsmen but would have done little to raise the reputation of sport in the eyes of its critics. The humorous exaggeration of supposedly real scenes, such as in John Nixon's *Brighton Races* (cat. no. 59) would, for example, have been seen as visual confirmation of the "folly and vice" which in the view of some attended sport.

Checklist

50.* Henry William Bunbury: *The Sporting Undergraduate*, 1772. Pencil, pen, ink & watercolor. 6 3/8 x 9 1/4 (162 x 235 mm.). PM. Egerton & Snelgrove: Bunbury no. 1 See p. 26

51. Henry William Bunbury: *Patience in a Punt* Watercolor. 8 x 12 3/8 (203 x 315 mm.). PM No. 62/5/22/3. Egerton & Snelgrove: Bunbury no. 6 See p. 26

52. John Collet: *The Joys of the Chase, or the Rising Woman and the Falling Man*, exhibited 1780. 16 x 23 1/2 (40.75 x 59.75 cm.). PM No. 3024. Egerton 102

53.* John Collet: *The Ladies' Shooting Poney*, 1780. Mezzotint, colored by hand. 12 7/8 x 9 7/8 (326 x 251 mm.). PM. Snelgrove: Collet no. 1

54. Isaac Cruikshank: *The Cuckold Departs for the Hunt, ca.* 1800. Pen & ink & watercolor. 6 3/4 x 8 7/8 (172 x 225 mm.). PM No. LGD 63/12/31/7. Egerton & Snelgrove: I. Cruikshank no. 1

55. After Isaac Cruikshank: *Cockney Sportsmen: Shooting Flying*, 1800. Etching by James Gillray, colored by hand. 7 3/4 x 12 (195 x 305 mm.). PM. Snelgrove: I. Cruikshank no. 1

56. After Isaac Cruikshank: *Cockney Sportsmen: Finding a Hare*, 1800. Etching by James Gillray, colored by hand. 7 3/4 x 12 (195 x 305 mm.). PM. Snelgrove: I. Cruikshank no. 1

57. H. F. B. Gravelot: *The Sporting Lady*, before 1773. Pen & ink & watercolor. 6 1/2 x 8 3/8 (165 x 213 mm.). PM No. LGD 64/8/7/24. Egerton & Snelgrove: Gravelot no. 1

58. Marcellus Laroon III: *Man and Woman with a Bag of Game*. Pen & ink over pencil with watercolor. 8 x 11 7/8 (203 x 301 mm.). PM No. 71/6/8/3. Egerton & Snelgrove: Laroon III no. 2 See p. 19

59.* John Nixon: *Brighton Races*, 1805. Pen & ink & watercolor. 20 x 26 3/4 (510 x 680 mm.). B1977.14.6235. Egerton & Snelgrove: Nixon no. 1 See pp. 25–26

60.* Thomas Rowlandson: *Bookmaker and Client Outside The Ram Inn, Newmarket*. Pen & ink & watercolor. 9 7/16 x 7 7/16 (240 x 192 mm.). B1977.14.327. Egerton & Snelgrove: Rowlandson no. 26 See p. 26

61. Thomas Rowlandson: *The Enraged Vicar*. Pen & ink & watercolor. 5 1/16 x 7 5/16 (128 x 186 mm.). B1975.3.59. Egerton & Snelgrove: Rowlandson no. 6

62. Thomas Rowlandson: *The Hunt Subscription*. Pen & ink & watercolor. 8 1/4 x 12 1/2 (210 x 317 mm.). PM No. 64/9/9/34. Egerton & Snelgrove: Rowlandson no. 12

63.* Thomas Rowlandson: *The Dinner*, 1787. No. 6 in a set of 6. Aquatint. 15 x 19 3/4 (381 x 502 mm.). PM. Snelgrove: Rowlandson no. 1 See p. 21

64.* Thomas Rowlandson: *Four o'clock in the Country*, 1788. Aquatint, colored by hand. 9 x 11 3/4 (228 x 298 mm.). PM. Snelgrove: Rowlandson no. 2 See pp. 11–12

65.* Thomas Rowlandson: *Four o'clock in Town*, 1788. Aquatint, colored by hand. 9 x 11 3/4. (228 x 298 mm.). PM. See pp. 11–12

66.* After Francis Wheatley: *The Amorous Sportsman*, 1786. Mezzotint by C. H. Hodges, colored by hand. 17 7/8 x 21 3/4 (453 x 552 mm.). B1977.14.14506 See p. 19

Section 5. *Diversification*

George Stubbs did not conceal his annoyance at his persistent label of "horse-painter," and might have found the title of "Animalium Pictor" accorded to him by Pierre-Étienne Falconet (cat. no. 68) to be only marginally less disparaging. The disrespect suffered by many sporting artists in the eighteenth century was partly responsible for the attempts at more 'elevated' subject matter which have been discussed in chapter III. The objects in the final section of the exhibition document this development.

Sportsmen's interest in combat between wild animals, philosophers' discussions of animals' independence from man and their ability to reason or to suffer, scientists' study of exotic species of animals, and the more general late-eighteenth-century concern with the depiction of extreme emotion were factors which helped to shape the precise nature of Stubbs's and his followers' movement away from conventional sporting ideals.

The results ranged from the calm presentation of mares and foals as self-contained beings (see the mezzotint after Stubbs, cat. no. 79, and Gilpin's derivative of the theme, cat. no. 69) to the portrayal of animals suffering from the onslaughts of their fellow creatures (cat. nos. 70, 72, 74, 75, 80) or of man (cat. nos. 71, 73).

Checklist

67. John Boultbee: *Grey Arab Stallion in a Desert Landscape*, ca. 1780–1800. 27 1/4 x 35 1/4 (69.2 x 89.5 cm.). PM No. 2545. Egerton 145

68.* After Pierre-Étienne Falconet: *Portrait of George Stubbs*, after 1769. Engraving by D. P. Pariset. 6 3/4 x 4 3/4 (172 x 121 mm.). PM.

69. Sawrey Gilpin: *Three Hunters in a Rocky Landscape*, 1775. 37 1/2 x 49 1/2 (95 x 125.5 cm.). PM No. 1196. Egerton 112 See pp. 31, 34

70. Sawrey Gilpin: *Horse Frightened by a Snake*, 1792. 11 3/8 x 14 1/8 (28.75 x 36 cm.). PM No. 1717. Egerton 116 See p. 33

71.* Sawrey Gilpin: *A Young Man with Horse, Hounds, and Dead Hare*, *ca.* 1795. Pen & ink & watercolor. 8 3/8 x 5 3/8 (213 x 136 mm.). PM No. LGD 72/12/14/127. Egerton & Snelgrove: Gilpin no. 5 See pp. 27–28

72. After James Northcote: *Lion and Snake*, 1799. Mezzotint by S. W. Reynolds. 18 3/4 x 23 1/2 (478 x 597 mm.). PM. Snelgrove: Northcote no. 4 See p. 33

73.* George Stubbs: *Freeman, the Earl of Clarendon's Gamekeeper, with a Dying Doe and a Hound*, 1800. 40 x 50 (101.5 x 127 cm.). PM No. 483. Egerton 97 See pp. 27–28

74. George Stubbs: *Horse Frightened by a Lion, ca.* 1790–95. 27 3/4 x 41 (70.5 x 104 cm.). B1977.14.73. Egerton 73

75.* George Stubbs: *Horse Attacked by a Lion*, 1770. 40 1/8 x 50 1/4 (102 x 127.5 cm.). On loan from Yale University Art Gallery. 1955.27.1 See pp. 32, 34

76. George Stubbs: *Tiger, ca.* 1769–70. 24 x 28 1/2 (61 x 72.5 cm.). PM No. 668. Egerton 83

77. George Stubbs: *Zebra, ca.* 1763. 40 1/2 x 50 1/4 (103 x 127.5 cm.). B1981.25.617. Egerton 74 See pp. 31, 34

78. After Stubbs: *A Tigress*, 1773. Mezzotint by J. Dixon. 18 7/8 x 23 (480 x 584 mm.). PM. Snelgrove: Stubbs no. 24. See also Egerton, p. 84.

79.* After Stubbs: *Brood Mares*, 1776. Mezzotint by Benjamin Green. 16 1/4 x 21 3/4 (414 x 554 mm.). PM. Snelgrove: Stubbs no. 11 See pp. 33–34

80. After Stubbs: *Horses Fighting*, 1788. Mezzotint by George Townley Stubbs. 17 7/10 x 23 3/8 (445 x 595 mm.). PM. Snelgrove: Stubbs no. 30 See p. 33

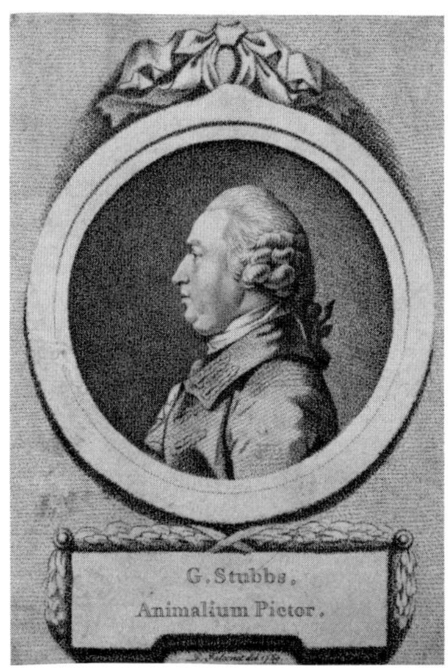

68. D. P. Pariset after Pierre- Etienne Falconet: *Portrait of George Stubbs*, after 1769

Other Objects

BOOKS

81. William Blane, *Cynegetica*, 1788. PM. Podeschi 67

82. Thomas Fairfax, *Complete Sportsman*, 1760. PM. Podeschi 53

83. William Gilpin, *Remarks on Forest Scenery*, 1791, vol. 2, pp. 266–67, *Passions of horses* by Sawrey Gilpin. Book DA 620. G49. 1794

84.* Julius Caesar Ibbetson sketchbook, 1793 to 1801. *Giraffe*, 1796, no. 25. Watercolor. PM. Egerton & Snelgrove: Ibbetson no. 14 See p. 34

85.* Charles Le Brun, *Characters of the Passions*, English edition, 1701. *Terrour*, engraving. Book NC 590. L4 See p. 32

86. *Nimrod's Songs of the Chase*, 1788. PM.

87. Col. Thomas Thornton, *A Sporting Tour Through the Northern Parts of England*, 1804. PM. Podeschi 81

88. *An Essay on Hunting, by a Country Squire*, 1733. PM.

SCULPTURE

89. Peter Scheemakers: *Francis, 2nd Earl Godolphin*, 1733. Marble. Height (with pedestal): 24 3/4 in. B1979.361.